VILLAGE CLUSTERS AND RURAL DEVELOPMENT

About the Author

Hariharan Ramachandran was Professor in the Department of Geography, University of Delhi (2005-12). He has earlier been Director, Institute of Applied Manpower Research, Planning Commission (2000-2005), and Executive Director, National Research and Resource Centre, LBS National Academy of Administration, Mussoorie (1997-2000). He has been the Associate Professor at the Institute for Social & Economic Change, Bangalore and then he was the visiting Professor at ISID, Delhi. He has authored/edited eight books and over 50 articles in national and international journals. He specializes in Urban/Regional Development, Quantitative Methods and Programme Evaluation. He has travelled across thirty countries relating to his professional activities.

Foreword

A CHALLENGING task faced in empirical research is to give concrete content to concepts which are easy to formulate but difficult to operationalise. Our experience in the Tumkur Project shows this to be very much the case in relation to the concept of "Cluster of villages". It was around the time I started the Tumkur Project in early 1977 that I had put forth the view-point that the small size and relative isolation of villages in India pose the major hurdle in organising rural development programmes which would be effective and pervasive. I was convinced that the answer to this hurdle lay in the integration of groups of neighbouring villages into viable "Clusters of villages" to form "Unit areas of development".* The idea seemed simple enough but my colleagues and I soon discovered in the field that it opens up a difficult area for empirical research posing several issues and questions few of which have received systematic attention so far.

Given this situation, my response has been to suggest a stepwise strategy starting out with the investigation of the relatively simpler questions raised by the idea of "Clustering of Villages". It seemed useful to begin by looking at the evidence on variations among neighbouring villages which could bring out their prevailing isolation from each other and provide clues on how integration among them could be promoted. This was followed by a study of the "Village Informant" level data on where the villagers go for employment, marketing and for rural amenities and services. The study was helpful in obtaining a rough idea about the contact zones of different types of villages and the extent to which neighbouring villages figure in the contact zones. Another approach to

* See my "Some Neglected Factors in Integrated Rural Development"—Address delivered on the occasion of the XVI Convocation of the Indian Agricultural Research Institute, New Delhi, 1977.

consider the question of clustering of villages was from the point of view of viability and effectiveness of the rural development institutions. This was one of the issues investigated in the Tumkur Project study on Panchayats. It was reassuring for me to find these studies bearing out my initial proposition that a cluster of villages needs to have an aggregate population of about 5000 covering a group of 5 to 6 neighbouring villages.

The present study by H. Ramachandran belongs to the more definitive phase of our work on the concept of cluster. Being a geographer and spatial analyst, he has been able to take a number of substantive steps towards making the concept operational. Before referring to them, I must make a brief mention of Ramachandran's perspective which stresses the importance for rural development of building up lateral contacts as against the dominant vertical contacts characterising the socio-economic relations encompassing the rural communities. It seems to me that in adopting this perspective Ramachandran makes a healthy departure from the traditional perspective of geographers and spatial analysts. It is from this fresh perspective that he tackles the question of how one may go about in delineating the clusters. The "nearest neighbour" criterion for delineation used by him avoids the mistake of attaching villages mechanically to their nearest higher order settlement as is usually done now by the geographers which could only perpetuate the prevailing alignments of rural contacts and relationships. Using this criterion, Ramachandran has delineated 287 clusters in Tumkur district. In my view, his population and area norms—4000 to 6000 population and maximum intra-cluster distance of 7 kms.—are reasonable which is also ture of the distinction that he draws between the rural clusters and those which seem to be located in zones of urban influence. I hope that the procedure for delineation developed by Ramachandran will find wider acceptance in the current programmes for organising the planning for rural development at the micro-level.

Having delineated the clusters, Ramachandran proceeds to examine the scope for intra-cluster interaction. Of particular relevance are his findings on rural amenities. He takes note of the biases and deficiencies in the prevailing pattern of road linkages which promotes vertical rather than lateral movement.

VILLAGE CLUSTERS AND RURAL DEVELOPMENT

H. RAMACHANDRAN

Foreword by
Prof. V.K.R.V. Rao

CONCEPT PUBLISHING COMPANY PVT. LTD.
NEW DELHI-110059

ISBN: 978-93-5594-877-9

Edition 2024

Published and Printed by

Concept
Since 1974

Concept Publishing Company Pvt. Ltd.
A/15-16, Commercial Block, Mohan Garden,
New Delhi-110059 (India)
T: 91-11-41101460
E: publishing@conceptpub.com, *W*: www.conceptpub.com

He also finds that the modest level of intra-cluster interaction occurring now rests on a limited base. Among the rural amenities that he considers only the middle school and the post office seem to be of the type conducive to intra-cluster interaction. Here, again, Ramachandran has something to offer to a wider readership. I hope the index of intra-cluster interaction worked out by him and his readable maps bringing out the wide variation in the index across the district of study would be useful additions to the techniques for analysing the locational aspects of rural amenities.

I must digress at this point to refer to the singular neglect by my own profession of economists of what may broadly be described as the "cost-benefit" aspects of rural amenities. It seems obvious to me that the norms of population and distance now being used in providing rural amenities need to be validated—and, if necessary, modified—in terms of explicit economic reasoning based on social costs and returns. I am convinced that a careful look at the economics of rural amenities and services from the broader development perspective would reveal substantial scope to bring a number of them down to the cluster level to enlarge the base for intra-cluster interaction.

To come back to Ramachandran's study, a line of investigation which needs considerable further work than he is able to put in relates to the question of how agro-climatic and socio-economic environments shape the features of clusters and give rise to significant differences in these features within the district, particularly as between its northern and southern parts. This is an important line of investigation focused on what may be called the "socio-economic determinants" of rural India. Ramachandran also mentions in passing that the effective planning for resource use would need a larger reference area consisting of a group of clusters. I hope that it will be possible for us to take up some of these issues in the other studies of the Tumkur Project though, quite clearly, no single group or project would be able to do justice to all the issues that one can identify.

Taking the study as a whole, it seems to me that Ramachandran's findings could be of considerable help in using the concept of cluster of villages in preparing the micro-level plans.

I take some encouragement from the fact that two states—Punjab and Karnataka—seem already to be experimenting with the idea of cluster of villages. It would be surprising if the compulsions of planning at the micro-level do not push more states along the same way. I feel happy at the thought that our work and studies in the Tumkur Project could be of some help to the planners and researchers in getting oriented through the 'cluster' concept to meet the new tasks emerging in the course of planning for rural development. It is in this context that I commend the present study to all those interested in the theme rural development.

Institute for Social and
Economic Change,
BANGALORE

V. K. R. V. RAO

20 May 1980

Acknowledgements

IT GIVES me great pleasure to put on record, on behalf of the Institute for Social and Economic Change and on my personal behalf, our sincere and grateful thanks to :

Government of Karnataka for financial assistance and for permission to avail of services of local staff;

Ford Foundation, Delhi and Sir Dorabji Tata Trust, Bombay for financial support and annual grants;

Bureau of Economics and Statistics and Government Computer Centre, Bangalore for access to data and to programming and computer services;

District, taluk and village officers—in particular, Block Development Officers, Extension staff and village-level workers—teachers and others who participated in and extended assistance during and for field work;

Academic, administrative and investigation staff of Tumkur Project;

Above all, the people of Tumkur district and its villages whose help and hospitality enabled us to reach the grass-roots.

Institute for Social and
Economic Change
BANGALORE

V. K. R. V. RAO
Hony. Director
Tumkur Project

Preface

THIS STUDY is a part of the larger ongoing research project on the Integrated Development of Tumkur district in Karnataka. Of necessity then, we start with a wide canvas of micro-level planning in a macro setting. Herein, the need for treating the territorial units as open systems and the necessity to promote inter-village interactions to pave the way for a fundamental strengthening of the basic structure and behaviour of the space economy is stressed. However, as we proceed the problem is narrowed down to the specific issue of defining the cluster of villages with reference to Tumkur district. In addition some aspects of the district's economy and infrastructure on the basis of the identified clusters are analysed. The findings of the study are then discussed within the theoretical format proposed and implications for planning are drawn.

During the tenure of this study, I have received considerable help and encouragement from various sources which I gratefully acknowledge :

Professor V. K. R. V. Rao for initiating me into this study and continuous encouragement.

Dr V. M. Rao for the benefit of discussions at various stages of the study.

Dr V. K. Tewari for various suggestions.

Miss A. K. Poovamma and Mr V. S. Deshpande, Research Investigators for unflagging enthusiasm and statistical assistance.

Mr B. G. Kulkarni for drafting the figures included in Chapter 1.

Mr S. Krishnamurthy and Mr N. K. Govinda Rao for efficient and prompt typing of the report.

Institute for Social and
Economic Change,
BANGALORE

H. RAMACHANDRAN
Human Geography and
Ecology Unit

December, 1979

Contents

List of Figures

List of Tables

1

Micro-Level Planning in the Macro Setting

Preamble

MUCH OF OUR models and programmes of development plans have remained segmental and partial and in many cases devoid of basic theoretical framework. Perhaps the most serious lacuna in micro-level planning is the treatment of the territorial unit as a closed system delinked from the macro processes.[1] The Government—bureaucratic machinery loaded with the problems of pragmatism in physical planning cannot understandably labour on these issues. Nor can they be expected to deal with abstract constructs. But the academics cannot ignore macro-processes while discoursing on micro strategies.

While it is true that territorial subsets of a national economic system are structurally distinct from neighbouring units—distinguishable by a set of attributes, such units also have "spatial links"[2] and are open to the impact of decisions, policies, price mechanism and a host of other networks of links. What, therefore, occurs in areas far removed and seemingly unconnected to small territorial units of study must fundamentally affect such units. Associated with this lacuna is the absence of historical method despite planning strategies being multi-faceted and inter-disciplinary. Although there is a glut in development planning literature wherein the oft repeated statement seems to be regarding its inter-disciplinary nature, history as a discipline is conspicuous by its absence. The historical and macro evolutionary processes of development have consequently been alienated from the current development strategies in vogue resulting in a mechanistic approach to the problems of planning for development. This has lead to a situation where the plans are based on faith—since their success or failure can be evaluated only after they are implemented.

Development literature is not however completely devoid of theoretical fibre. We have among other models the centre-periphery, the circular causation, growth pole, export base model and so on. The logic of these abstract constructs of the West when stretched to real world situations of the third world only breaks. While this is not the place to proceed with a comprehensive review of these constructs and their failure when applied to countries of the third world we note the failure of these models.

Geographic inertia, multiplier effects, export surplus, diffusion of growth impulses which are the stock in trade of a large part of the literature on development are not tenable. The 'magic export base' is found to act as an instrument of drain rather than investment both at intra-national and inter-national levels. Large scale public investment in the basic industrial/ 'generative' sector leaves the neighbourhood virtually untouched.[3] This observation is not however true, the heavy industrial centres (armed with the 'multiplier' and 'percolation' effect) of Bhilai, Rourkela, Jamshedpur etc., are drawing on their neighbourhood resources, to be ultimately drawn into the metropolitan economy. Simultaneously, the resource rich neighbourhood of such centres remains one of the most under-developed regions. The degree of under-development is caught irrespective of well or ill conceived criteria and by the most crude to the most sophisticated methods of measurements. An analysis of railway freight patterns has convincingly brought out the control of metropolitan economy on the resource base of such areas.[4] Also, firstly, whatever impulses are generated are impounded within the 'cores' and the part that does percolate diffuses hierarchically to other 'minor cores' rather than to the neighbourhood hinterland. Secondly, the peripheries in the third world are not in a condition to absorb the residual flows if any. These experiences take away much of the *raison d'etre* of the various received theories. The surface charm of these models and the explicit faith shown by their propagationists has led to a number of programmes of development that were implemented voraciously. Such programmes and their effects are reviewed in a later section.

Under these circumstances the emergence of the Latin American school led by Frank, Furtado, Sunkel, etc., comes as a relief to the study of problems of development in the under-developed countries.[5] Within the context of the present theme, Frank's distinction between under-development and lack of development is fundamental.[6] Failure to recognise this distinction has resulted in treating under-development as a stage in the development process and consequently the practice of placing different territorial units (district, States) in a national or nations in a global development scale. As Frank observes, "This relation between development and under-development is not a comparative one", and therefore cannot be measured with the same yardstick. They are structurally different, albeit related. This, then, is the benefit of hindsight. Replacing "under-developed" by "developing" has at best aided the failure of differentiating under-development and lack of development. Such semantic games, however, satisfy the taste of the "under-developed lot" and stand for the tact of the "developed lot".

Rural Urban Relations

Since the term rural refers to a segment of the society while development in general refers to society in toto, the non-rural component cannot be ignored, and in fact, the characteristics of and happenings in the non-rural segment are to a large extent responsible for the development of under-development in the rural segment. The process of rural urban relations is fundamental in rural planning. In the macro-setting the concept of metropole-hinterland relations in India are extensively dealt with in a number of writings.[7] We also have evidence at the national level of the suction mechanism operating in the country wherein the resource rich areas export their primary produce either directly to the metropole or after processing in 'growth poles' located in them. Such growth poles act as satellites to the metropoles and aid in the flow of resources from the rural hinterland to the metropolitan economy. The spoils of this process are mutually exchanged by the urban centres.

There is no reason to believe that such a process is not

operating at lower levels and with smaller urban centres of the regional settlement sub-systems. The unique position of the urban places where the redistributive authority has come to be vested plays a key role in this suction process.[8]

The nature of the relationship between the rural and the non-rural segments of a society is one of unequal exchange of goods and services. Within the hierarchical arrangements of human settlements of varying sizes, the pattern of interaction is essentially composed of vertical links. While hierarchical arrangement of human settlements within a space economy seems to be a natural development of settlement systems, the pattern of vertical links is not so. The dominant vertical links are more pronounced at the lower rungs of the hierarchy as compared to settlements of higher orders where lateral relationships are more discernible.[9] Under unfavourable placement, rural settlements that occupy the lower levels of the settlement hierarchy, continually lag in attracting developmental efforts. In the positivist framework of analysis this growing gap is attributed to the lack of economic viability and thresholds for developmental efforts. It is not that the explanation of poverty given by Lipton in terms of urban bias in the investment pattern is unimportant but more crucial is the kind of relations between the urban and the rural sector.[10] The fundamental process of the integration of the two segments is the exchange of surplus production. The necessary requisite of this act—the price making and redistributive authority vested with the urban market consequent upon expansion of production base has got decentralised and shared between hierarchically arranged multiple centres of power. In this connection it has been observed that the "overbearing dominance of the metropolitan centre upon the primary sector cannot be explained unless we assume that the territorial economic base is so designed as to endow those centres with super ordinate authority to redistribute".[11]

The above observations give us a vantage point to look at the development programmes in the country, particularly those geared to bring about rural development of some form or the other.

Earlier Programmes and Plans

Soon after independence the community development programme with accent of Panchayati Raj, cooperative and agricultural development was launched. Under this programme the country was divided into development blocks each consisting of about 100 villages and provided with extension specialists in agriculture, animal husbandry, social education etc. This was supplemented with health services, family planning, small scale and cottage industry, marketing and related facilities. The block headquarters located in rural surroundings were designed to function as nodes through which rural development programmes could be carried out. In due course each block set up an elected advisory body.

The programme did not come up to expectation. Its failure is explained as follows, in a number of papers on development planning in India. The villages were grouped haphazardly; neither the quantity nor the quality of the services provided at block level were sufficient to meet the rural community needs, benefits accrued to the land-owning communities without touching the poorer sections of the population; the programme as a whole was largely oriented towards welfare rather than development.

Realising the 'ineffectiveness' of the community development programme in transforming rural India, a new strategy for agricultural development known as the Intensive Agricultural District Programme (IADP) with the technical cooperation of the Ford Foundation in India was started. Under this programme (started in 1960), a few districts with favourable physical conditions for agriculture were selected for intensive efforts, involving provision of the agricultural inputs, marketing facilities and administrative and institutional devices deemed necessary for modernisation and commercialisation of agriculture. Gradually the IADP has been extended in a less intensive manner to about 2/5th of the Indian districts, under the name of Intensive Agricultural Area Programme (IAAP).

The new programme has been credited with the initiation of a "green revolution" in India. Despite its effectiveness in productivity in some districts of Punjab and delta districts of Andhra Pradesh, the overall performance of IAAP districts has been no better than non-IADP districts.[12] The new seed fertiliser technology is biased towards irrigated areas and has given rise to increased disparities in interpersonal and inter-regional income in rural areas.

Along with these agricultural development programmes, pilot research projects in growth centres of the Government of India in collaboration with the Ford Foundation in India were launched in 1969 to be operated for five years. Under this project, block plans were prepared for about 20 blocks. A hierarchy of service centres was defined and general service centre plans were made (the reliance on growth centre approach and 'percolation' cannot go unnoticed).

However, whereas the western countries had reached the social transformation threshold needed for accelerated industrialisation, the situation is quite different in countries like India. Besides, the growth centres are expected to perform three kinds of functions in the Indian context, as service centres, centres of secondary activities and as points of social interaction and of diffusion of innovations.[13] The assumption of promoting such centres is based on the idea that what is needed for propagating development is implanting some propulsive industries. In ignoring the macro processes (some of which have been outlined above) our efforts at developmental planning are like filling water in a bottomless bucket. We draw attention particularly to the explanation of the failure of these programmes by various government agencies and social scientists. This reasoning is only superficial and plugging the gaps raised therein futile.

With these theoretical considerations and a review of ongoing development programmes, we proceed to look at the study area—Tumkur district of Karnataka. Tumkur—the district headquarter itself is a town of over 70,000 population that perhaps falls in the third level of the hierarchic order of the national urban system.[14] The district as a whole must be viewed as a part of the hinterland of the Bangalore metropolitan economy.

Background to the Study Area

Detailed information covering a large range of facets (social and economic)—are available elsewhere.[15] It is therefore unwarranted to lengthen this report by duplicating such information base. Nonetheless, some brief basic information is given here for ready reference. The intentions of this section are only to highlight the various developmental problems facing the district and the symptoms of under-development of this backward district.

Tumkur district is situated between 12.45° and 14.29° North latitude and 76.29° and 77.30° East longitude (Fig. 1.1). The district has a common boundary with Chitradurga and Ananthapur districts in the north, Mandya district in the south, Kolar and Bangalore districts in the east and Hassan in the west. Pavagada taluk is a bit removed from the rest of the district and juts into Ananthapur district of Andhra Pradesh. With a north-south dimension of about 154 kilometres and an east-west of 110 kilometres, the district spans an area of 10550.9 sq. kms.

Two hill ranges which run parallel to each other are conspicuous relief features. The first in the eastern part of the district passes through Pavagada, Madhugiri, Koratgere and northern parts of Tumkur taluk. The second passes through the western part of the district through Chiknayakanahalli, Sira and Gubbi taluks (Fig. 1.2). A third cluster of hills is also to be noticed in the middle and southern parts of the Kunigal taluk. Shimsha, Vedavathi and Jayamangali are the important rivers, which rise from the hills and feed some of the tanks. Among the tanks, Boranakanive and Marconahalli reservoir are important ones.

The Tumkur district is populated by 1.63 million people (5.56 per cent of Karnataka's population) of which 12 per cent constitute urban population as per 1971 census. The share of the urban population is considerably low when compared to the State (25 per cent of the population is urban in the State). The population of the district is distributed in 12 urban centres and 2452 villages. Small towns are more frequent in the district accounting for a substantive proportion of urban population (Table 1.1).

Towns are generally service towns with tne larger segment of the workers engaged in the tertiary sector as compared to that of Karnataka. Small villages are numerous about 77 per cent being villages with less than 1000 people. The average size of a village is 527 as against 751 for Karnataka as a whole

Location of Tumkur District

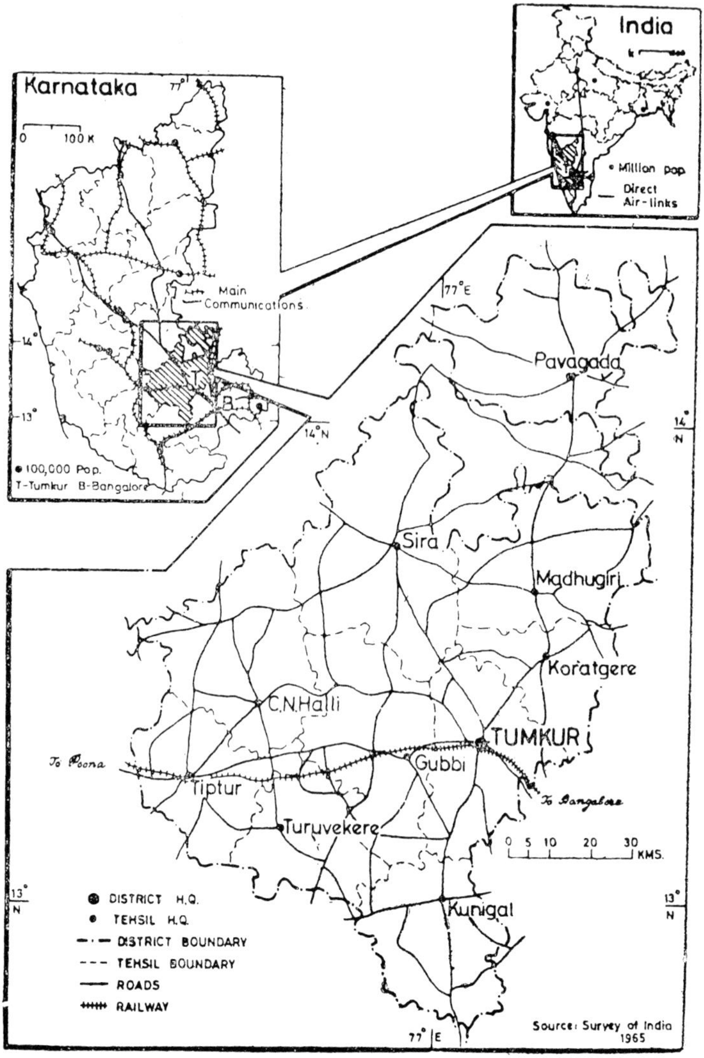

FIG. 1.1

(Table 1.2). Consequently about 75 per cent rural population of the district live in villages with less than 1000 people (the corresponding value for Karnataka being 38 per cent), and

Physiography of Tumkur District

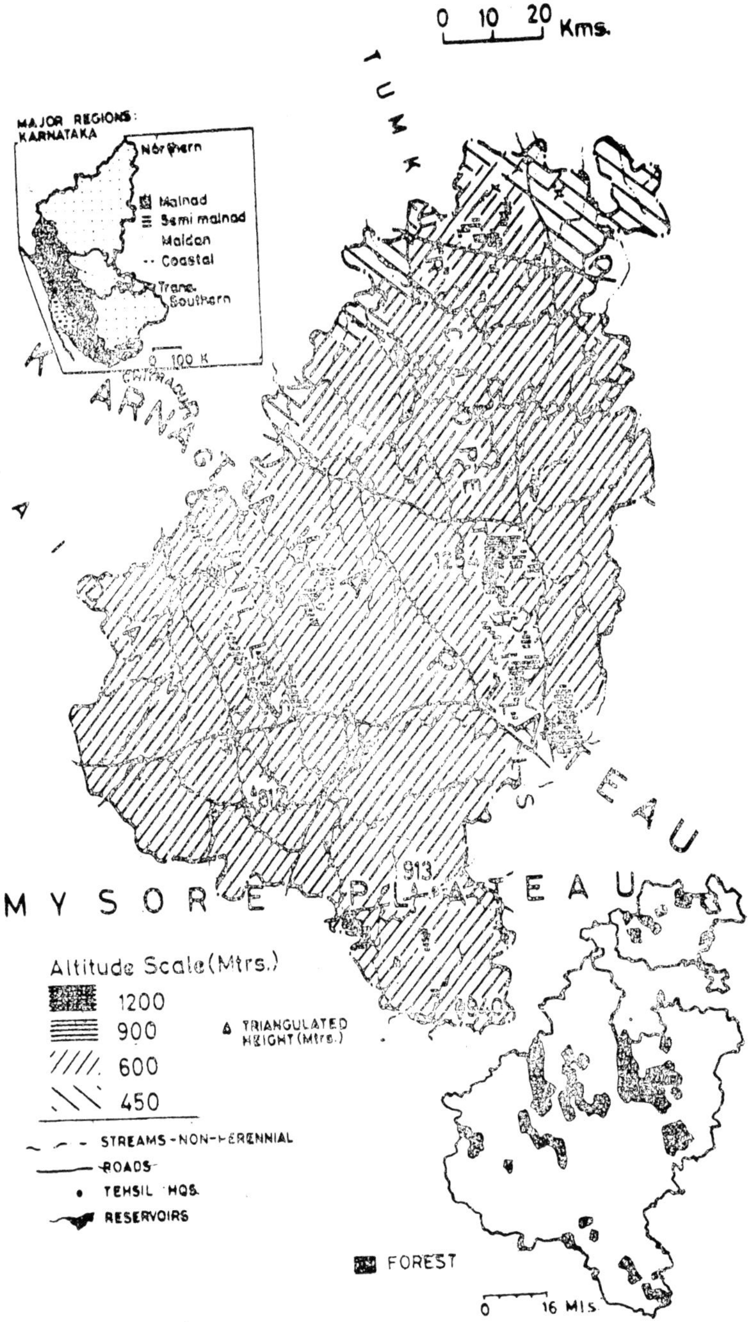

FIG. 1.2

TABLE 1.1

Size of urban centres (1961-1971) and functional category

Name of the Town	Population 1961	Population 1971	Functional category 1961 Census	Functional category 1971 Census
1. Ammasandra Notified area (NAC)	—	1577	—	Industry
2. Chiknayakanahalli	10,375	13,061	Industry-cum-Primary activities	Primary Activities-cum-Industries
3. Gubbi	8,543	9,537	Primary Activities-cum-Industry	Primary Activities-cum-Industry services
4. Karatgere	4,301	5,794	Primary Activities	Primary Activities-cum-Trade & Commerce
5. Kunigal	10,566	13,437	Primary Activities-cum-Services	Industry-cum-Primary activities-cum-Trade and Commerce
6. Madhugiri	11,275	14,117	Services-cum-Industry-cum-Primary Activities	Services-cum-Trade and Commerce-cum-Primary activities
7. Pavagada	5,913	9,004	Primary Activities-cum-Industry	Primary activities-cum-Services-cum-Transport Storage & Communication
8. Sira	15,408	18,299	Industry	Industry-cum-Primary Activities-cum-Trade & Commerce
9. Tiptur	15,558	22,592	Industry-cum-Services-cum- Trade & Commerce	Trade and Commerce-cum-Industry-cum-Service
10. Tumkur	47,277	70,476	Services-cum-Industry	Industry-cum-Trade and Commerce-cum-Services
11. Turuvekere	4,983	6,536	Primary Activities-cum-Services	Industry-cum-Primary activities-cum-Services
12. Y.N. Moskote	4,790	6,177	Industry	Industry

Source : District Census Hand Book, Tumkur District, Census of India, 1971.

TABLE 1.2

Distribution of villages by size—1971

S. No.	Taluks	Size Category										
		Uninhabited		500		500-1000		1000-2000		2000+		Total
1.	Chiknayakanahalli	18	(8)	124	(53)	61	(26)	23	(10)	8	(3)	234
2.	Gubbi	50	(14)	187	(54)	76	(22)	26	(8)	7	(2)	346
3.	Koratgere	26	(18)	151	(60)	52	(21)	20	(8)	2	(1)	251
4.	Kunigal	23	(7)	162	(52)	86	(27)	37	(12)	5	(2)	313
5.	Madhugiri	45	(14)	161	(50)	70	(22)	30	(9)	14	(4)	320
6.	Pavagada	9	(6)	40	(28)	43	(30)	41	(28)	11	(8)	144
7.	Sira	25	(10)	116	(47)	58	(23)	38	(15)	12	(5)	249
8.	Tiptur	10	(4)	135	(59)	59	(26)	22	(10)	4	(2)	230
9.	Tumkur	43	(11)	198	(50)	112	(28)	34	(9)	8	(2)	395
10.	Turuvekere	24	(10)	127	(52)	67	(28)	21	(9)	4	(2)	243
11.	Tumkur District	273	(10)	1401	(51)	684	(25)	292	(11)	75	(3)	2725

Source : District Census Hand Book, Tumkur District, Census of India, 1971.
Figures in parentheses represent percentage to taluk total.

14 per cent in villages above 2000 (corresponding value for the State is 34 per cent). Within the district Pavagada taluk appears as a separate class with an average village size of 899 and 8 per cent of its villages above 2000 size (also see Fig. 1.3.).

Distribution of Settlements

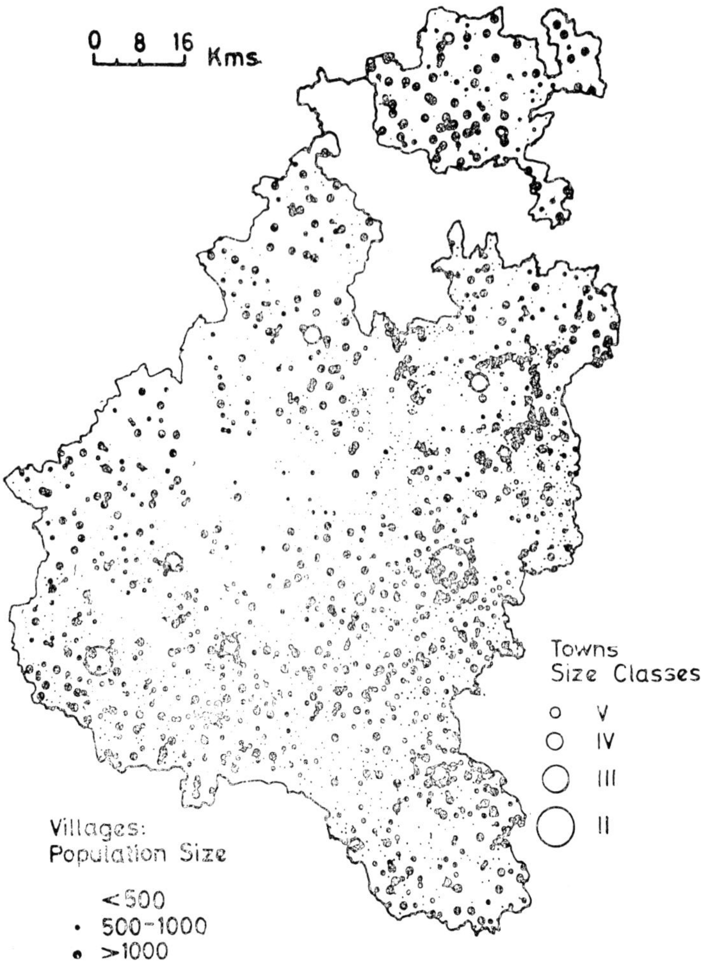

FIG. 1.3

Koratgere on the other hand has the least average village size with 394 and only 1 per cent of the villages with more than 2000 people (Table 1.2). Compared to other districts in Karnataka, villages in the Tumkur district are in closer proximity to each other. The density of villages per 100 sq. kms. is 26 in Tumkur while it is only 16 in rural Karnataka.

The size attributes also give us an indication of the future course of urbanization. The prospects of increase in the number of towns in the district is bleak, since large villages which are likely to become towns are few.[16]

The district is characterised by continuous out-migration. Migrants born outside the district accounting for 7.64 per cent as compared to 10.86 per cent in the rest of Karnataka. Job opportunities are therefore less lucrative in the district than in the rest of the State. This is also corroborated by the sex ratio of the migrants which indicate short distances 'marriage migration' that are more dominant in an analysis of migration streams.[17]

Primary activities continue to be dominant in the district with income from agricultural and allied activities accounting for 68 per cent in 1960-61 to 74 in 1970-71 and 80.4 per cent in 1974-75, whereas the relative share of industry and mining has come down from 11.2 per cent through 8.6 to 5.7 respectively. Correspondingly, workers in these sectors have also reacted similarly. Whereas workers in agriculture and allied activities increased from 83.6 per cent in 1961 to 86.65 per cent in 1971, industrial workers came down from 9.2 per cent to 5.76 per cent.

Only 14 per cent of the net area sown is irrigated. The intra-district variation is not very high ranging from Tiptur recording 4 per cent to Madhugiri recording 24 per cent. Under such conditions, dry crops of coarse grains—ragi, jowar and millet dominate the cropping pattern. Pulses are uniformly encountered in all the taluks averaging around 15 per cent of gross cropped area. Cash crops like groundnut (Koratgere, Madhugiri and Pavagada) and coconut (Chiknayakanahalli, Tiptur and Turuvekere) are restricted to few taluks. The district has also a large strength of cattle, sheep and goats. However, pasture and grazing land are grossly inadequate.

Only 13 per cent of the grazing and pasture land required are at present available.

We have already seen the minor role of industries in the district's economic activities through income figures. Only one large scale industry is located in the district at Ammasandra, a cement factory employing 866 permanent workers. However, some 600 small scale registered factories of which a little more than 50 per cent engage 5 or more workers (accounting for about 3000 employees) and 17,333 small establishments in traditional industries and handicrafts that account for the bulk of industrial workers in the district (about 47,000 in 1974) are operating in various parts of the district.

Having prepared the ground with theoretical considerations and a brief background of the study area, we proceed in search of an indigenous model which perhaps answers parts of the question raised here. However, what is perhaps most needed in development planning in India is an understanding of the political economy of regional development that forms the basis for micro-level planning.

REFERENCES

1. At best in a very few studies the territorial unit has been placed within a framework of larger urban hinterland or a larger geographic/physiographic region.
2. The term 'spatial' is used to designate links that are not only with contiguous/regional units, but open to non-contiguous units as well.
3. B. Chattopadhyay and Moonis Raza, "Regional Development, Analytical Framework and Indicators", *Indian Journal of Regional Science*, VII, 1975, p. 11-34.
4. See for example, S. Chakraborty, "Urban Economic Base : A Contemporary Indian Experience," paper presented at the Indo-French Seminar on problems of urban growth, New Delhi, 1978, and Nira Ramachandran, "Commodity Flows and the Regional Organisation of the Indian Economy", unpublished Ph. D. dissertation, Centre for Regional Development, Jawaharlal Nehru University, New Delhi, 1979.
5. A. G. Frank, *Capitalism and Under Development in Latin America*, Monthly Review Press, N.Y., 1967. C. Furtado, *Development and Stagnation in Latin America : A Structural Approach*, New Haven, 1965. O. Sunkel, "Integration capitaliste Transactionale in Disintegration Nationale en Amerique Latine," *Politics Etrangere*, 6, 1970.

6. A. G. Frank, *On Capitalist Underdevelopment,* Oxford University Press, Bombay, 1976.
7. Among these within the context of our theme we refer to S. Chakraborty, op. cit., B. Chattopadhyay and Moonis Raza, op. cit.
8. S. Chakraborty, op. cit.
9. This is evident from an analysis of passenger bus connection patterns—V.L.S. Prakasa Rao, et. al., "Urban Systems and the Regional Economy", paper presented at Indo-French Seminar on Problems of Urban Growth, New Delhi, 1978, or of the Railway Freight Patterns, Nira Ramachandran, op. cit.
10. M. Lipton, *Why Poor People Stay Poor : Urban Bias in World Development*, Temple Smity, London, 1977.
11. S. Chakraborty, op. cit.
12. R. P. Misra, et. al., "*Regional Development in India : A New Strategy*", Vikas, New Delhi, 1974.
13. Ibid.
14. V.L.S. Prakasa Rao, et. al., op. cit.
15. A series of mimeographed profiles of various taluks of the district has been brought out by the Tumkur Project staff, ISEC, 1978.
16. P.N. Mari Bhat, Population, "Education and Employment in Tumkur District, 1921-71 : A Census Analysis", The Tumkur Project, ISEC, Bangalore (Mimeo), 1978.
17. Ibid.

2

The Concept of Cluster and Cluster Formation

HAVING DISCUSSED the untenability of development models that are based on the concepts of diffusion, we have no alternative but to search for an indigenous model that fits in within our political economy, and social ethos and runs parallel with the macro processes. This calls for much more than a change of few parameters and usher in fundamental changes in the philosophy of our planning. In fact the frequency with which concepts and theories are out-dated is a measure of research progress, particularly when the old ones have outlived their usefulness.[1] It is in this background that we view the concept of a village cluster.

The Concept

While the idea of cluster of villages in various contexts has been aired albeit, nebulous, within the framework of rural development the concept has recently been given a concrete shape.[2] The basic idea is to treat the numerous small villages of the country as a community of a smaller number of clusters of contiguous villages. Such a treatment alone, however, is no solution to any of our rural problems. But we may be in a position to convert such clusters into an instrument of fundamental change by promoting intracluster interactions, community feelings, simultaneously dissipating the growing upward linkages and providing a more viable unit area of development in our blighted rural sector.

We view village clusters above the individual village (instead of central village/small town) as a strategy to strengthen lateral links and to dissipate growing vertical links in the settlement systems. Such clusters while providing greater viability and threshold for developmental efforts will also create for themselves a greater bargaining power in bringing about reciprocity in exchange of goods and services. There is no apparent dichotomy between the concept of settlement hierarchy and that of village clusters. Within the hierarchical settlement system, a grouping of villages at lower levels is visualised for the purpose of consolidation and better bargaining power (for attracting developmental efforts) by encouraging intra-cluster integration through interactions which would act simultaneously as a balancing force against the continuing upward links that are encountered in the settlement systems.

Such clusters would warrant that inter-cluster disparity be minimised so that the clusters are of same level and intra-cluster diversity be maximised in order to facilitate interaction.[3] Interactions take place because of diversity of situation aided by adequate network for interactions, through transportation facilities.[4]

The programme for rural development offers substantial scope for bringing neighbouring villages together to share common amenities and to constitute large sized institutions like Panchayats and co-operatives, and in its turn effective coming together of neighbouring villages would improve the rural environment and make it more conducive for economic growth, rural diversification and emergence of viable rural institutions.[5]

Understandably, whereas regional planners' efforts have not come down to the village as a unit, village studies are confined to single villages, and get no opportunity to look at a village as a part of a larger neighbourhood and hence provide little help in looking at this problem.

To improve the delivery system of rural amenities for rural development is a welfare measure and does optimise the allocation of scarce resources. But on its own it is merely a planning of infrastructure and has very little to do with the much needed changes in the basic structure of human habitat and the pattern of links between them. Indian villages have had a long tradition of living together in a workable system until the free market monetised pricing system disrupted it, and brought them within the fold of the urban/metropolitan economy. This process in itself is not pejorative, but the built in suction mechanism in this process is. The hierarchic arrangements and the pattern of transport route networks, that connect the villages to the nearest highway linking them to the urban centres, go hand to hand with this exploitative system.

An unemotional sector-space-resource planning must be supplemented by more passionate application of the rural community idea. The planning for rural amenities at cluster level can get above the welfare level to reach a developmental role. Land transactions, lease, ownership, kinship links and contacts usually end up with those of neighbouring villages. There is therefore already some semblage of neighbouring village contacts. Higher level functions would, however, continue, to need larger grouping consisting of more than one cluster. A cluster of contiguous villages which in course of developmental efforts and planning must acquire the characteristics of a single community.

Intuitively the cluster as an aggregate has to be large enough to overcome small size barrier and dissimilar components. Technical/operational problems in delimiting the clusters in the light of several criteria which need to be kept in view are physical features, existing pattern of intervillage communication and contacts and prevailing grouping of villages for the purpose of Panchayat, co-operative society, etc.

Earlier Attempts at Cluster Formation

The necessity for identifying a unit area for physical planning at sub-block/extra village level has grown sporadically in various parts of the country. However, among the few such formulations there is an apparent lack of clarity both at the levels of concept and mechanics of grouping villages into clusters. It is necessary that we review such attempts before we labour on the mechanics of grouping villages into clusters.

A note on block level planning for full employment released by the Regional and District Planning Unit of the Government of Karnataka delves briefly on the necessity of grouping 20 or 30 villages into a cluster, it does not proceed beyond that in the direction of empirical grouping.[6] Following regional concepts, the note suggests requirements of homogeneity (in attributes like soil types, water logging, irrigation, areas with under-developed infrastructure, etc). It also feels that if the blocks and agricultural assistant's circles are homogeneous in the above mentioned characteristics they may be conveniently treated as groups of villages. It is also brought out that about 20-30 villages are likely to occur within a radius of 4 to 6 miles, within which employment has to be generated for the unemployed villagers.

Under the integrated Rural Development Programme for 1977-78 to 1981-82 of the Development Department of the Government of Punjab, the idea of cluster of villages has been taken a step further than the one mentioned by the Karnataka Government.[7] For purposes of planning, the State has been divided into 500 units of an area of 100 sq. kms. each, by super-imposing a grid on the State. Each such unit area would have about 20 to 25 villages. Initially a cluster of five contiguous villages in each of 117 blocks in the State is to be taken as the unit for planning and development. The purpose for such clustering of villages according to the report is to bring the planning process nearer to the field level and to make the scheme more relevant to the problems and potentialities of the selected areas and its people. The exercise still does not depart from the concept of central village and growth centre theory (focal point village is also an integral part of the clusters of villages). The report believes that the focal points would lead to the generation and dispersal of economic development in the periphery. Despite the introduction of the cluster concept, the basic philosophy of growth centre planning remains the solid foundation for this plan. About 302 crores of rupees are expected to be spent on this programme.

For the limited purpose of studying the characteristics of a group of continuous rural settlements, villages have been clustered around a set of random points.[8] Some 200 odd clusters have been identified in the district—the basic criteria being geometrical contiguity. From the operational point of view the selection of random points around which clusters are defined (the concept of focal point/central village is altogether abandoned) leads to the omission of villages in some cases and overlaps in others. The clusters thus derived, then, do not necessarily cover all the villages in a study area and the method does not yield a unique solution, i.e., different sample points will result in different clusters.

On Defining a Cluster of Villages

Within the conceptual framework posed in the previous section, we may identify the requirements of a cluster, and then add other criteria from the pragmatic point of view.

1. The group of villages in a cluster should be contiguous.
2. The population size of the cluster be big enough to attract locational decisions of amenities.
3. The villages in a cluster be diverse so that an atmosphere for inter-village interactions be created.
4. The grouping of villages into clusters should follow a simple procedure so that the mechanics are easily understood and applied, and the method gives a single solution and unique group of villages in a cluster.
5. Resulting clusters should be capable of being aggregated further for purposes of planning economic activities. To this extent a common basic feature of physical homogeneity be maintained.

The reflection on these criteria leads us to the conclusion that not all of them could be met at a single stroke under all situations of space economy. While requirements (1) and (2) in most cases can be met, it is not possible to insist that the third requirement be met simultaneously. However, existing literature on cluster characteristics strongly suggests the possibility of achieving this without specific effort[9]. On the basis of randomly selected villages and their adjoining settlements, it has been demonstrated that the villages show marked differences in a number of criteria like levels of literacy, scheduled caste population, occupational structure and the like. This is also corroborated in this study in a later section. Requirement (4) is entirely from practical considerations and can be insisted upon under all circumstances. Requirement (5) however paves the way for consolidation at a higher level and is possible to meet along with all other criteria since structurally (physical attributes like relief, climate, soil, natural resources) a large number of contiguous clusters of villages are likely to be homogeneous as a rule. At best this would call for minor relaxation of either requirement (2) or (4) (i.e., leaving room for subjective adjustments keeping in view the structural/physical characteristics of the constituents of a cluster). The principle of least effort suggests that once the conditions of complementarity and transferability are satisfied, neighbourhood interactions will take place. Thus since one of the major purposes of cluster level units is promotion of inter-village interactions, the principle of clustering must be based on the concept of nearest neighbour.

Grouping Villages into Clusters

We now proceed with an illustration of the method adopted to group the villages into clusters. A hypothetical set of village locations with their population size is given (Fig. 2.1.A). Each village may be linked to its nearest neighbouring settlement (Fig. 2.1.B). We may refer to this linked group of villages as primary clusters. Each settlement will have atleast one nearest neighbour and may itself be nearest to more than one other settlements. Obviously the smallest of the primary clusters then, will have only two villages. At this stage, we may introduce our limits of population and distance conditions. In the present analysis a population size of a cluster has been fixed between 4 to 6 thousand and distance range is limited to 7 kilometres (i.e., the farthest village in a cluster does not exceed 7 kilometres). If the primary clusters satisfy these limits we may treat them as the final clusters. However, in a number of cases these conditions will not be satisfied. For these cases we may then link a primary cluster to another primary cluster (nearest to it) and match against population and distance limits. The process may be continued till the population and distance criteria are satisfied by all clusters (Fig. 2.1.C).

Since the two constraints are independent of each other in many cases only one of them may be satisfied. Deviations from these norms are likely to occur because of the presence of urban centres which encourage bypassing of middle order centres and large villages and thus collapse inter-village interactions. Secondly, the nature of spatial distribution of settlements also disturbs the population and distance constraints posed.

To offset the disturbances created by these urban places, we have marked off a radius of 10 kms in the case of 11 of the 12 towns in the district and a radius of about 15 kms in the

FIG. 2.1 *Grouping of Villages into Clusters*

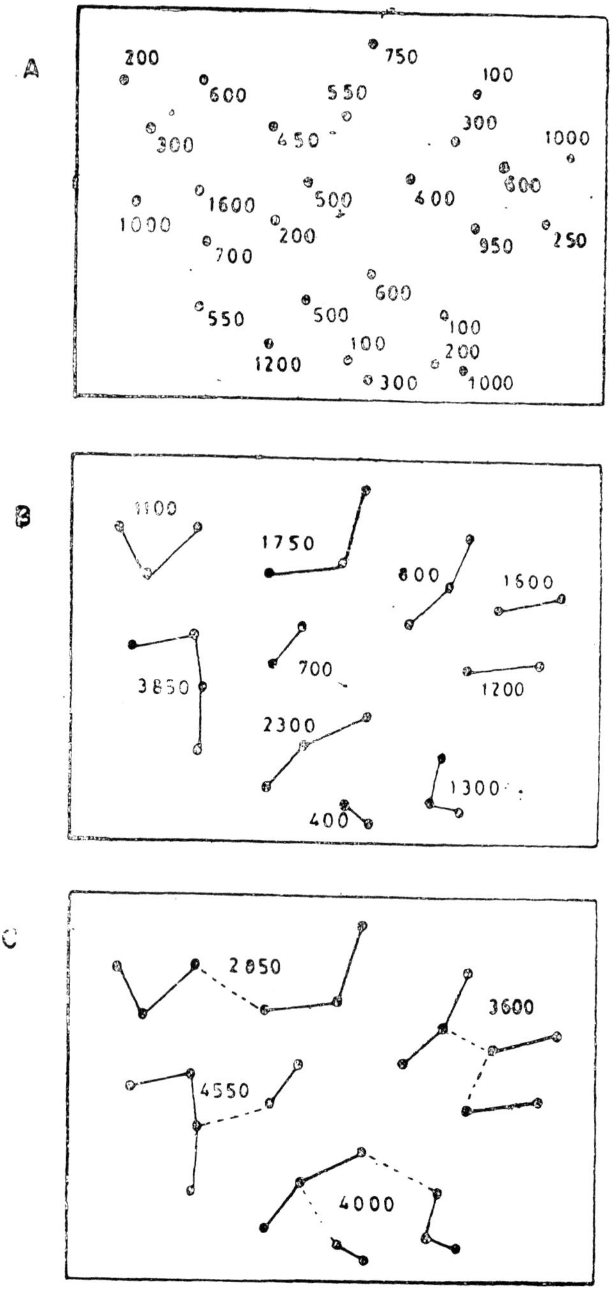

case of the district headquarters (Tumkur) which is a Class II town with a population of over 70,000.[10] Applying the method outlined above the district has been divided into 202 clusters of which 12 are urban influence areas. The urban influence areas are also divided into 87 clusters keeping the same population and distance norms. However, the deviations from the norms in the clusters within urban influence areas may be considerable. Thus the 2452 inhabitated villages of the district are treated as 277 clusters of which 87 clusters are in urban shadow area.

A list of villages included in each of the clusters is given in *Appendix I* and a map delimiting the clusters is shown in Fig. 2.2. Since the distribution of villages (Fig. 1.3) brings out that some areas are characterised by large villages dispersely spaced and other small closely spaced villages, a number of clusters indicate either below 4000 population or above 6000 population (Table 2.1).

TABLE 2.1

Distribution of clusters by population size classes and zone of urban influence

Total Population of cluster	Beyond urban influence zones		Within urban influence zones	
	Number	Percentage	Number	Percentage
< 2000	1	0.53	12	13.80
2000–4000	39	20.53	36	41.37
4000—6000	84	44.20	25	28.73
6000—8000	48	25.27	8	9.20
8000+	18	9.47	6	6.90
Total	190	100.00	87	100.00

The modal class in the case of clusters beyond the urban influence zones is 4000—6000, accounting for 44 per cent of clusters, which was the limit posed by delineating the clusters. The impact of urban centres on the size of the villages is brought out by the fact that the most frequent size in the urban influence areas is small i.e., 2000—4000 which accounts for 41 per cent of such clusters. Since the spatial distribution for

Village Clusters in Tumkur District (Clusters in Urban Influence Zone are enclosed by bold lines)

FIG. 2.2

villages of various size affects the size of the clusters, we have also shown the clusters in various population size categories in a map (Fig. 2.3).

Population Size of Clusters (Unshaded Clusters represent the Set Population Size Norm of 4000-6000)

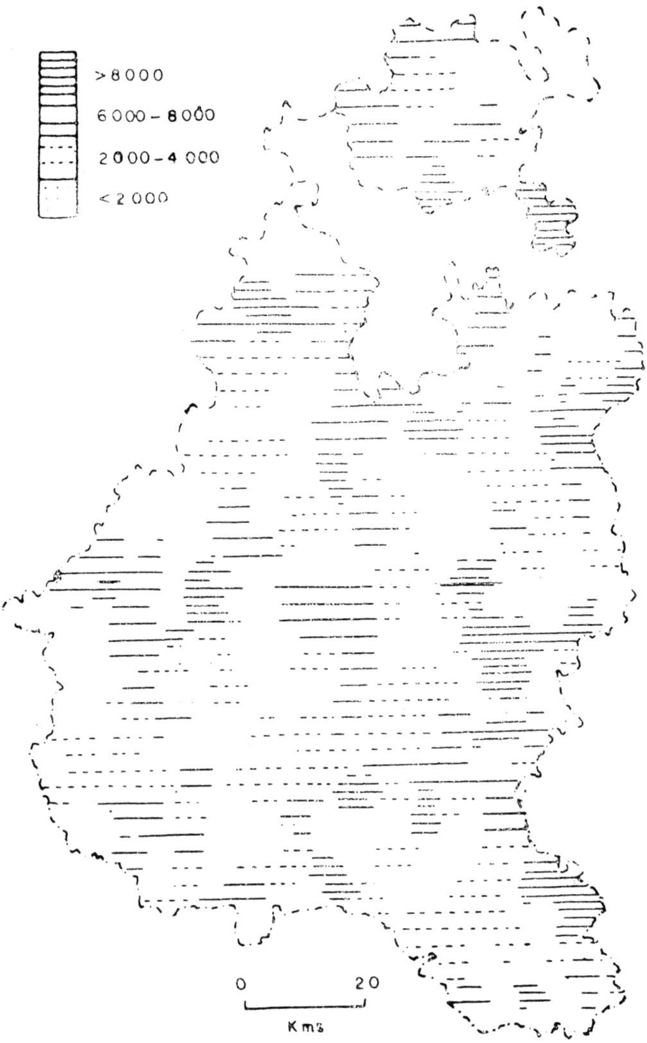

FIG. 2.3

Since many of the villages are small-sized and closely located in parts of Kunigal, the population size of the clusters is generally less than 4000. On the other hand, parts of Koratgere, characterised by large villages located in close proximity with each other, record clusters with large population, though the inter-village distances are not large. Thirdly, large villages with dispersed location pattern of Sira taluk produce clusters with large populations wherein inter-village distances are also great. Fourthly, many of the clusters in the urban influence area are smaller in population size except in the case of the Tumkur town influence zone, wherein a number of clusters are large-sized (above 8000 population).

Related to the population size of the clusters are the differences in the number of villages in them (Table 2.2). In both cases, whether the clusters are within the urban influence zones or beyond them, the most frequent occurrence is villages numbering between 6—10 in a cluster.

TABLE 2.2

Distribution of clusters by size and zc e of urban influence

Size of cluster (villages)	Beyond urban influence zones		Within urban influence zones	
	Number	Percentage	Number	Percentage
< 6	19	10.00	31	35.64
6—10	107	56.32	44	50.58
10+	64	33.68	12	13.78
Total	190	100.00	87	100.00

In this category fall 107 clusters beyond the urban influence zone and 44 in the urban influence zones. A smaller number of villages (i.e., less than 6) in a cluster is found in a larger number of cases (31) in the urban shadows and fewer in other areas (19), whereas larger number of villages (i.e., more than 10) are more frequent in clusters beyond urban influence areas (64) than clusters in urban influence areas (12). Within this general distribution we find some extreme cases. For example, twenty-four villages are aggregated in one case to form a cluster to add up to a population size of 5806 in Tumkur taluk. On the other hand, in another cluster located in C.N. Halli, three villages add up to give a population size of 8280. Similarly within the influence area of Turuvekere town, in one cluster 18 villages (located close to each other) when aggregated, result in a population of 17,511 whereas in another cluster within the same area 5 villages are aggregated to add up to the cluster population of 829.

All this is to bring out the fact that in spite of some general norm regarding the size of the cluster, there may be many cases which violate such conditions, because of local characteristics. Thus even within the same framework of analysis the possibility of more than one norm can also be considered to accommodate local variations, particularly settlement pattern and population distribution. Nonetheless, we may stress that the search for optimal size values is not really the ideal pursuit. The distance limit based, both for delimitation of clusters, and for demarcating urban influence areas, as also the population thresholds are arbitrary based largely on intuition and findings of several studies on micro level planning. The method used here can be applied with any other limits.

The spatial analysis of the economic base, distribution of central functions and intervillage interactions is based on the clusters that have been formed in this chapter. As we proceed we may note differences in the behaviour of clusters within and beyond the urban influence zones.

REFERENCES

1. R.T. Holt and J.E. Turner, *The Political Basis of Economic Development*; East-West Edition, Van Nostrant Reinheld Co., N.Y. 1970.
2. V.K.R.V. Rao, "Some Neglected Factors in Integrated Rural Development", XVI Convocation Address, Indian Agricultural Research Institute, New Delhi, Jan. 1977.
3. We draw attention to the fundamental distinction between the terms 'disparity' and 'diversity'. The distinction has been succinctly put as follows : "Differences in initial conditions of resource endowments largely of a natural or physiographic character . . . . . constitutes the substance of inter-regional diversity . . . . . Regional disparity denotes the failure of a region to exploit the development potential of its initial resource endowments . . . . . and is comprised

of factors which are not natural or physiographic but human, institutional and historical, socio-political and/or economic technological". B. Chattopadhyay and Moonis Raza : "Regional Development : Analytical Framework and Indicators", *Indian Journal of Regional Science*", VII, 1975.

4. E.L. Ullman, *American Commodity Flows*, Washington University Press, Seattle, 1957.
5. V.M. Rao : *Rural Development and Village : Perspectives for Planning for Development*, under publication, Sterling, New Delhi, 1980.
6. Government of Karnataka, District and Regional Planning Unit, Economic Adviser's Division, Planning Department, "A Note on Block Level Planning for Full Employment", (Mimeo—undated).
7. Government of Punjab, Development Department, "Integrated Rural Development Programme—Project Report for 1977-78 to 1981-82" Chandigarh.
8. V.M. Rao, op. cit.
9. Ibid.
10. Although more sophisticated methods and criteria have been used for delimiting such urban shadow zones, it is assumed that a simple distance limit would suffice for the purposes of the present study.

3

The Economic Base : Sectoral and Spatial Dimensions

RURAL ECONOMY is essentially agriculture-based in all the third world countries, though it need not be so. Even within the primary sector the preponderance of agriculture is apparent whether we consider the population dependent directly on it for its livelihood or the income that accrues through agricultural activities. In Tumkur district about 75 per cent of the income generated is from the primary sector, 17 per cent from the tertiary sector and only 8 per cent from the secondary sector as per 1970-71 data. Of the four hundred and seventy-three million rupees generated from the primary sector, over 94 per cent of the income is accounted for by agriculture. Among the workers in the primary sector over 96 per cent are engaged in agricultural activities as per 1971 census. Within this background of the district's economy we probe for further details of the structural and spatial dimensions of primary, secondary and tertiary sectors of the economy.

The Primary Sector

Agricultural economy is strongly rooted to the land. This root to the land is a fundamental distinction between a rural and an urban economy. The direction of development indicated and the limitations posed by the physical environment on the agricultural economy must therefore be understood and analysed in order to grapple with the problems of the rural economy.

Physical Environment

The district is generally an open tract with undulating plains lying between an altitude of 2000 to 2800′ above mean sea level. Except for patches of high tracts as mentioned earlier (Fig. 1.2) wherein peaks reach up to almost 4000′ the undulating plains prevail with general lie of the land tilting northwards. Consequently taluks of Pavagada, Sira are at lower elevation than the rest of the district. Forest patches are therefore confined to these ranges covering the central parts of the district (northeastern parts of C.N. Halli, northern parts of Gubbi, southern parts of Sira, north-eastern parts of Tumkur, western parts of Koratgere and southern parts of Madhugiri taluks). Smaller patches of forest are also to be noticed in Pavagada, Kunigal and Tiptur taluks (Fig. 1.2, inset). The forests are characterised by trees of dry belt.

No perennial rivers drain the district. However, numerous small streams fed by rainfall cover all parts of the district. Of these, Shimsha and Jayamangali are the important ones (Fig. 1.2). Many of these in their turn feed the numerous tanks and reservoirs that are littered all over the district.

The temperature regime of the district permits agriculture throughout the year. Although no meteorological stations are located in the district, the interpolated temperature values from adjoining districts, places the district's hottest season in April with 40-41°C (104-106°F) and the coldest in December with 9-10°C (48-50°F). The northern parts of the district covering Sira and Pavagada are hotter than the rest of the district.

About 45 days on an average in an year are rainy, that decreases towards north. The highest rainy days occur in Tumkur (54 days) to the lowest in Pavagada (35 days). Similarly the average rainfall of 687.9 mm (27.08″) decreases from south to north and from west to east. Much of the rainfall is confined between May and November, October has the heaviest rainfall and the rainfall in the two months of October and November amount to about 28 per cent of the annual rainfall. The average annual rainfall as recorded in different Taluks are as follows :

Pavagada and Sira	20-22″
Koratagere, Tiptur and Madhugiri	22-25″
C.N. Halli and Turuvekere	25-26″
Gubbi, Kunigal and Tumkur	28-31″

The cold weather rain (December-March) are scanty and are not much needed for the standing crops. However, they help to keep up pasture supply and replenish the tanks. The heavy short spell of rain during April (accompanied by storms) are important to the cultivators for preparation of land for sowing before the south-east monsoon.

The semi-dry conditions then keep the water table low. The water table is normally at 25-30′ except in river basins where they rise to 10′ below the surface.

Consequent upon such climatic conditions the soils are hard and poor with the exception of lands irrigated by tanks, spring channels and *nalas* which are loosened and are fertile. Soils truely are a micro regional element that change in their quality, type and texture within a matter of few metres at times, in spite of having common parent geological condition. Terrain conditions, exposure to winds and other climatic conditions produce a number of changes and cause variations within short distances. On the other hand details of soil types are rare to come by at such micro levels. For example, of the net area sown (1975-76) in the 245 randomly selected sample villages (10 per cent random sample in each of the ten taluks) only 23 per cent of the area was covered by soil surveys during 1970-71 to 1975-76.[1] The proportion of area covered in Tumkur taluk is 57 per cent and it is less than 2 per cent in Koratgere taluk. Soil classification and types are difficult to obtain with reference to the village aggregates.

The parent material of Archiean complex in the form of crystalline schists, granite, gneisses and newer granite results in red soils (the ragi soil) in southern and western parts of the district and black soil in the northern parts. The proportions of different soil types in each taluk are tabulated in Table 3.1.

In Tumkur, Kunigal and Sira soils are red and loam which are well drained but poor in lime content. With manure and irrigation red soils and red-loams with their quality of good drainage suit a variety of crops that can be grown on them. Black soils have high water holding capacity and hence are suitable for cotton, groundnut, jowar and tur.

The physical environment then indicates a dry cultivation culture for the district and consequently the district has for a long time remained a dry crop cultivator. While temperature

TABLE 3. 1

Talukwise soil types in Tumkur district

('000 acres)

Sl No	Taluk	Red soil	Gra-velly soil	Sandy Soil	Clay loam	Red loam	Black soil	Sandy loam	Clay soil
1.	C.N. Halli	—	71.92	40.50	—	60.13	6.08	—	—
2.	Gubbi	200.00	80.00	—	—	—	—	—	1.00
3.	Koratgere	—	—	0.20	—	10.00	—	20.00	3.00
4.	Kunigal	65.25	233.67	8.39	—	—	—	—	—
5.	Madhugiri	50.00	—	—	8.00	—	25.00	—	—
6.	Pavagada	20.00	—	—	85.00	—	0.04	25.63	9.40
7.	Sira	—	25.00	11.00	355.44	—	8.00	5.00	—
8.	Tiptur	100.06	—	—	—	—	2.50	39.50	22.00
9.	Tumkur	118.36	24.18	—	—	34.04	5.20	61.10	20.00
10.	Turuvekere	54.20	15.00	10.00	10 00	75 49	1.50	—	16.00

Source : Based on Tumkur District Gazetteer.

conditions allow agriculture throughout the year the lack of water is the chronic problem. Thus areas with irrigation and assured water supply are constantly under crops round the year. The ratio of area under wet to dry cultivation is to the tune of 1 : 10.

Ironically, since the district does not have large perennial system the small short distance drainage of seasonal streams and the tanks and the reservoirs are rainfed, only those parts of the district which record heavier rainfall can be brought under irrigation. Significant expansion of area under irrigation is possible only if irrigation through canals from major river system are made available from adjoining districts.

The Land Use

With this physical background we may pass on to seek patterns of land utilisation. Among the various uses the land is put to, it is obvious that net sown area occupies the largest proportion (51%) in the district. Of these the drier north record lesser proportions of land under cultivation than the wetter southern tract (Table 3.2). Pasture land follows this with 12 per cent of the geographical area. The proportion of land under forest in various taluks may be read along with the map (Fig. 1.2, inset). Current and other fallows record about 11 per cent. Again the drier parts in the north including Pavagada, Sira and Madhugiri taluks obviously tend to record higher proportions than the southern parts. Proportion of fallow land then, is directly related to the environmental conditions.

Extent of Irrigation

Only 14 per cent of the net area sown is irrigated (Table 3.2). Turuvekere, C.N. Halli and Tiptur have least proportions of irrigated area. Of these, two taluks also record lowest proportions of area sown more than once. The major source of irrigation is the numerous tanks accounting for 50 per cent of the total irrigated area followed by wells which account for 45 per cent of the irrigated area.

Clusterwise distribution of proportion of irrigated area to gross cropped area is mapped in Fig. 3.1. The striking feature of the pattern of distribution is the occurrence of highly irrigated areas in patches, and not in continuous stretches. This is

TABLE 3.2

Land utilisation (1975-76)

Taluk	Percentage to total geographical area								
	Forest	Culti-vable waste	Pas-tures/ Grazing land	Land under trees	Current fallows	Other fallows	Net sown area	Net irri-gated area to net sown area	Areas sown more than once
1. C.N. Halli	7.29	17.40	5.24	2.42	2.91	2.20	50.42	4.40	1.43
2. Gubbi	8,27	2.35	14.45	2.32	6.62	4.10	45.38	11.07	4.19
3. Koratgere	4.90	3.74	16.78	0.16	6.50	3.34	51.85	18.30	1.95
4. Kunigal	6.65	12.88	10.76	0.11	1.42	1.79	54.69	20.60	4.90
5. Madhugiri	2.93	8.67	9.82	2.03	6.40	3.85	47.24	24.00	4.33
6. Pavagada	4.32	4.75	9.80	0.31	17.06	7.10	48.00	15.10	4.07
7. Sira	3.51	6.15	15.71	1.61	8.36	2.50	43.29	18.60	3.40
8. Tiptur	0.78	6.87	12.80	5.77	0.69	1.21	62.88	4.20	3.97
9. Tumkur	0.80	1.77	9.92	3.05	11.82	4.09	56.66	17.70	4.72
10. Turuvekere	0.74	1.72	18.34	1.00	1.57	7.49	60.99	6.60	0.79
11. District Total	4.22	6.77	12.10	1.82	7.00	3.79	50.91	14.00	3.12

only to be expected, since the major sources of irrigation are tanks and wells and not canals and streams. However, one does find a linear stretch of high proportion of irrigated area in Tiptur taluk running north-south that records 20-50 per cent gross cropped area under irrigation. A much smaller patch of higher level of irrigation is also to be noticed in clusters lying in the southern parts of Kunigal taluk. Clusters located in northern parts of Sira taluk and entire Pavagada record low proportion of irrigated area.

A frequency table (Table 3.3) showing number of clusters against various percentage classes of irrigated area brings out preponderance of poorly irrigated tracts. We can also notice from the table the higher level of irrigated area in the clusters in urban influence zones as compared to other clusters. Exception to this are urban shadow clusters in Pavagada and Turuvekere taluks (Fig. 3.1).

TABLE 3.3

Distribution of clusters by percentage classes of irrigated area

Percentage area irrigated	Urban influence areas		Beyond urban influence areas	
	Number	Per cent	Number	Per cent
< 5	7	8	19	10
5—10	21	24	45	24
10–20	29	34	66	35
20—30	18	21	42	22
30–50	11	12	16	8
50+	1	1	2	1
Total	87	100	190	100

As observed earlier, the proportion of irrigated area tends to be higher in areas of higher rainfall. Thus, the southern parts of district generally record higher proportions. This is largely explained by the major source of irrigation (tanks and wells) that is directly dependent on the rain that falls within the area.

Irrigated Area as per cent of Gross Cropped Area

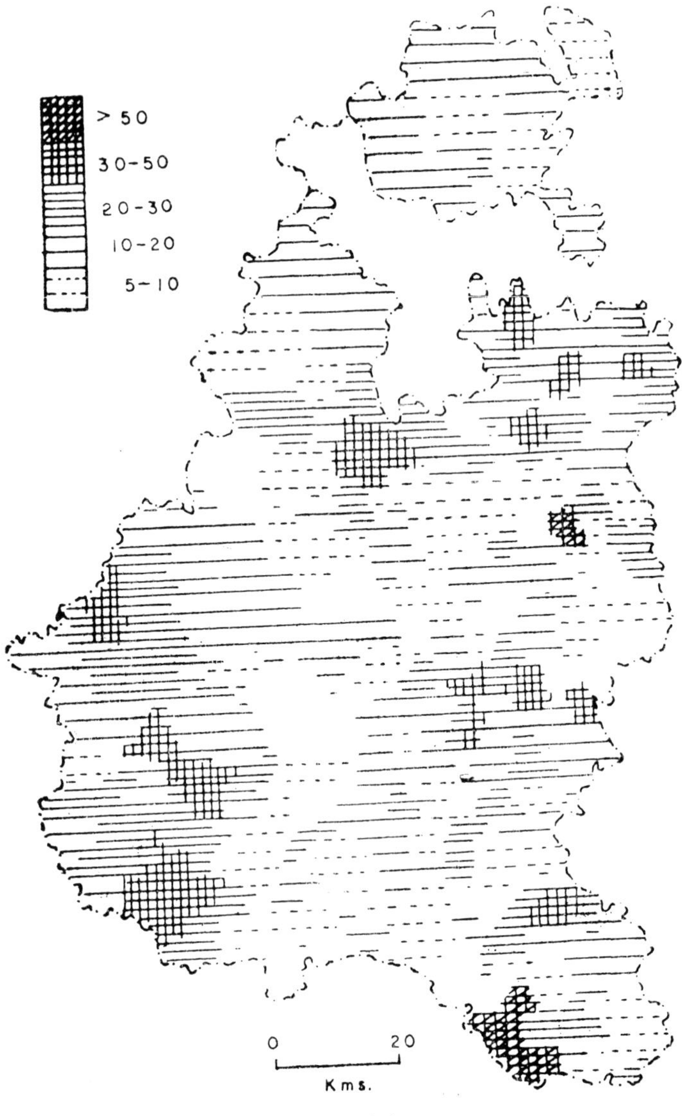

FIG. 3.1

Patterns of Cropping

Under this physically trying conditions, it is apparent that hardy drought resistant crops will have to be favoured. Consequently ragi occupies a major part of the cropped area, roughly accounting for a third of the net sown area, and is found in conspicuously lower proportions in the northern taluks—Pavagada, Sira and Madhugiri. Pulses including tur (*togari*) are more ubiquitously raised, though nowhere does it occupy a dominant position. All other crops are much more restricted in their spatial distribution (Table 3.4).

TABLE 3.4

Talukwise distribution of major crops*

Per cent area to gross cropped area

Taluks	Rice	Ragi	Jowar	Minor Millet	Pulses	Ground-nut	Coco-nut
1. C.N. Halli	—	22.4	—	—	10.3	—	19.7
2. Gubbi	11.1	40.7	—	—	18.5	—	—
3. Korat-gere	—	23.7	—	—	16.4	19.8	—
4. Kunigal	14.0	37.0	—	—	13.1	—	—
5. Madhugiri	24.4	—	—	10.7	16.6	16.7	—
6. Pavagada	10.8	—	11.6	12.7	19.7	25.8	—
7. Sira	—	—	—	14.9	13.3	—	—
8. Tiptur	—	30.0	—	—	12.1	—	27.0
9. Tumkur	17.0	46.7	—	—	18.7	—	—
10. Turuve-kere	—	39.6	—	—	16.7	—	17.0
11. District Total	9.6	25.4	—	8.3	15.6	7.7	6.9

*Only those crops which record more than 10 per cent of gross cropped area of taluks are included.

Of particular interest is the large proportion of land under coconut in a few taluks. We have to make do with this data on coconut since village level data on acreage under coconut is not available.

We now bring out clusterwise distribution of major crops. The data is based on village-wise crop data available with the

Bureau of Economics and Statistics and pertain to the year 1970-71. Ten major crops are recorded. Since considerable problem is encountered in matching this data with other sources particularly with reference to gross cropped area, net sown area and total geographical area, the proportions of individual crops have been computed as percentage to the area under these ten major crops. Consequently the percentage shown for different crops are much higher than the taluk level and district level pattern presented earlier. However, despite this problem, the relative position of different crops vis-a-vis the various territorial units (clusters) are maintained.

Since ragi is the major crop both in terms of intensity of production as well as with reference to its ubiquitous distribution we start with an analysis of its spatial distribution. It is the major food crop and a staple food to much of the rural population and grown extensively in the district. Being one of the hardiest crops it is well suited for dry farming and can grow under conditions of very low rainfall. It does withstand severe drought conditions and revives after a good shower. Red soil, sandy loam, light red soils are most suited for the crop. Manuring attains importance since plant food is absent from these soils. The straw from the crop forms an excellent fodder. The crop is sown in early/mid July and the sowing can be postponed till August if rainfall conditions warrant. Ragi sown in this season (*hain*) takes longer to mature but gives better yields. Throughout the district mixed cropping is practised wherein *togari* (tur) or *avare* (bean) is sown along with ragi. This is largely to reduce the risk of failing and delayed rainfall. When rainfall conditions are unfavourable for ragi, *avare* and *togari* grow better and vice-versa. Ragi is normally rotated with groundnut, fodder and jowar.

Clusterwise distribution of acreage under ragi is mapped in Fig. 3.2. Except for four clusters in Pavagada taluk, ragi occupies more than 5 per cent area devoted to the major crops. Almost all the clusters in southern parts of the district record above 50 per cent of area under ragi, thus giving a dominant place to the cultivation of ragi. Many of the clusters in Madhugiri, Koratgere record between 30—50 per cent area.

Ragi occupies minor position in the northern parts of Sira and entire Pavagada taluk with less than 30 per cent of the

Area under Ragi as per cent of Area under Major Crops

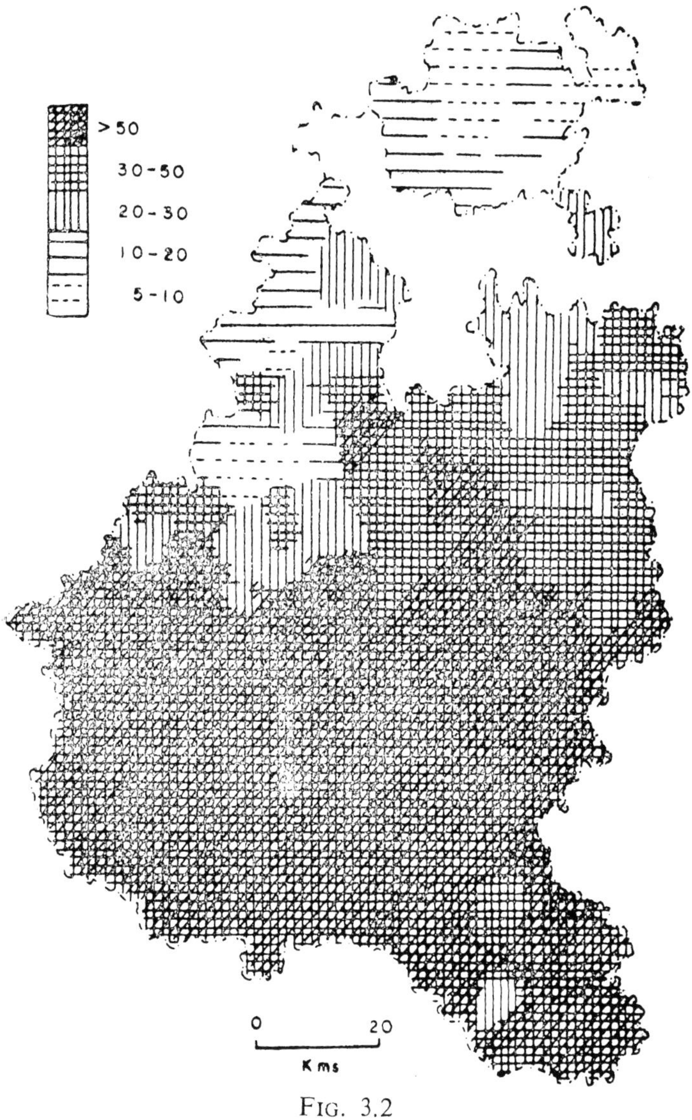

FIG. 3.2

area under major crops. A band of heavy concentration of ragi in the southern parts, a medium intensity area in the central parts, and low proportions in the northern parts of the district is the prevailing pattern.

Of the 277 clusters delineated in the district, 175 clusters record more than 50 per cent area, 47 between 30 and 50 per cent and 22 clusters show area under ragi between 20 and 30 per cent and only 33 clusters record less than 20 per cent area.

Since the distribution patterns are based on village aggregates at cluster level, it is necessary to look at the inter-village variations. For this purpose, a selected number of clusters are considered. A ten per cent systematic areally stratified sample of clusters are chosen from the district separately for clusters in urban influence area and others. Coefficients of variation in perctenage area under ragi between the villages in those clusters are tabulated in Table 3.5.

TABLE 3.5

Intervillage variation in per cent area under Ragi

No. of villages in the sample cluster	Percentage area under ragi	Coefficient of variation
12	5–10	63
13	10–20	55
19	20–30	58
36	30–50	31
198	50+	26

The intervillage variation is generally small in most of the clusters, irrespective of the location of clusters within or without urban influence area (hence the breakup is omitted in Table 3.5). Larger coefficient of variation is noticed where percentage class has lower value. In fact, the larger the proportion of acreage under ragi, the lesser the intra-cluster variation.

Following ragi, rice is the most important staple food grown in practically all taluks of the district, mostly under tanks and well irrigation. Physiologically rice adapts itself to a variety of conditions of both climate and relief. Only the varieties differ with differing physical environment under which the paddy is raised and consequently agricultural practices also vary. Paddy grows best on clayey loams to clays that turn soft when puddled. It also grows on alluvial and light sandy soils and several other variations subject only to constant flooding, uptil 10-15 days before harvest. It thrives best under conditions of high temperature and humidity. Varieties are available that can be grown under rainfall as low as 14″ to as high as 200″. The main limiting factor of this semi-acquatic plant is adequate and continuous supply of water.

The kharif season begins during June, July or August and ends in November to January. Rabi season begins during January and February and ends between May and July. Much of the paddy in the district is grown in summer. The *Punaji* or dry cultivation of paddy is resorted to in several parts of the district. Under this, the *Barabhatta* variety once sown receives very little attention for the following two months after which water is made available. Paddy straw is used as an important fodder though less nutritious than ragi straw.

In tracts possessing irrigation facilities from wells and tanks, rice is rotated with sugarcane, plantain and other irrigated garden crops. In dry areas ragi and groundnut or unirrigated pulses are grown in rotation with paddy.

Since the water requirement for paddy cultivation is considerable, clusters in the south-eastern tract that receive higher rainfall and consequently higher proportion of irrigated area through wells and tanks show concentration of acreage under rice (Fig. 3.3). In extreme southern patches of Kunigal taluk, rice acreage record proportions of over 30 per cent of the area devoted to major crops, including a cluster where rice is the dominant crop with over 50 per cent area.

Unlike ragi, a large number of clusters show less than 5 per cent area under rice. Such areas are conspicuous in the western parts of the district. However, when compared to the spatial distribution of the various crops (that follow) rice is most widespread within the district. The most frequent percentage class of area under rice is 10-20 per cent (94 clusters) followed by 5-10 per cent (89 clusters). As we go north and west in the district, area under rice thins down, following the pattern of irrigated area and rainfall conditions. Ironically, it is in these parts—Pavagada for example—where the yield of rice tends to be higher. In Pavagada the yield is between 18-20 quintals per acre, whereas parts of Tumkur, Madhugiri and Koratgere

Area under Rice as per cent of Area under Major Crops

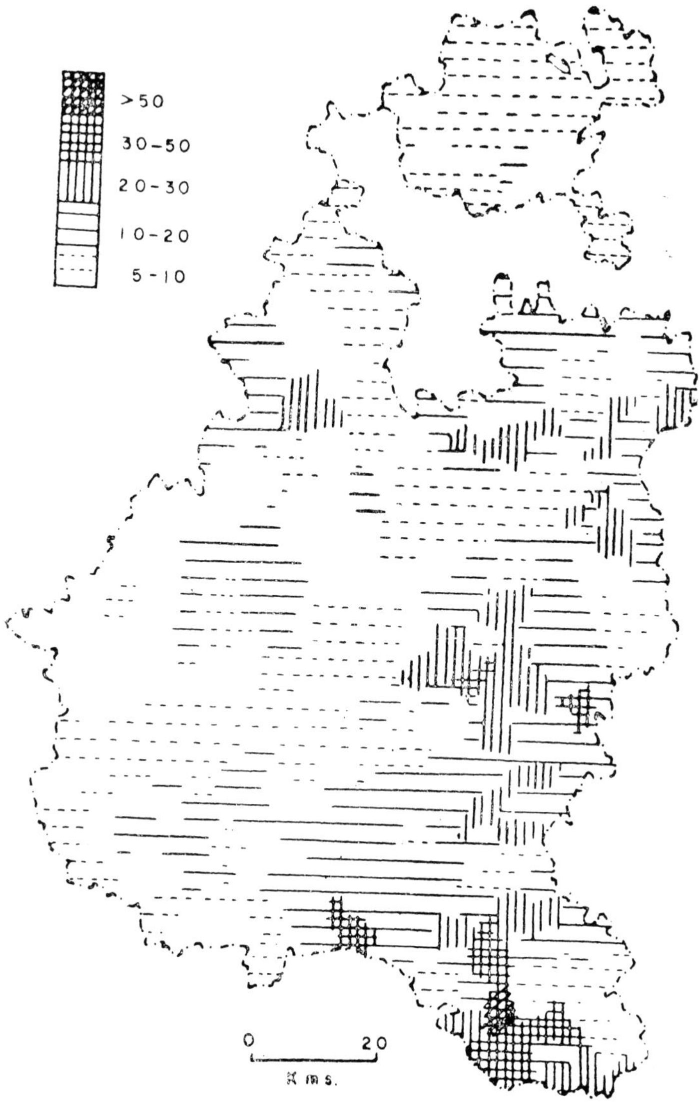

FIG. 3.3

record 15-18 quintals and the rest of the taluks only 10-15 quintals per acre.

Intervillage variations of area under rice is large (Table 3.6). Again the possible explanation is the variations in irrigated area within the clusters. Clusters where rice occupies lesser area show more variations as compared to those clusters which record higher proportions of rice.

TABLE 3.6

Intervillage variation in per cent area under rice

No. of villages in sample clusters	Percentage area under rice	% Coefficient of variation
34	Below 5	107
73	5-10	106
142	10-20	102
33	20-30	74
18	30-50	70

Jowar is a dryland food crop which grows under conditions of low rainfall and can withstand drought conditions. Neither excessive soil moisture for any length of time nor prolonged drought are conducive for raising the crop. It is a quick growing crop and secures good yields and is also used as fodder. The crop is largely raised on black soils although jowar also grows on red and light-red soils. Best crops are however grown in clay loam, and consequently dry stream beds and low lying fields without water stagnation give best yields. Sowing is normally undertaken between May and July and harvest between September to November. In Tumkur district the most common rotation with jowar is cotton and groundnut. Early jowar is followed by horsegram and Bengalgram. The main season ragi crop is grown in the second year. It is also grown as a mixed crop with oilseeds (castor, sesamum), minor millets and vegetable crops.

The physical conditions needed for cultivation of jowar, particularly soil conditions, then, indicate concentration in Pavagada and parts of northern taluks of the district. Thus Pavagada, Sira and parts of Madhugiri taluk record higher proportions of acreage under jowar. Clusters in the eastern and central parts are devoid of this crop. In western taluks a

Area under Jowar as per cent of Area under Major Crops

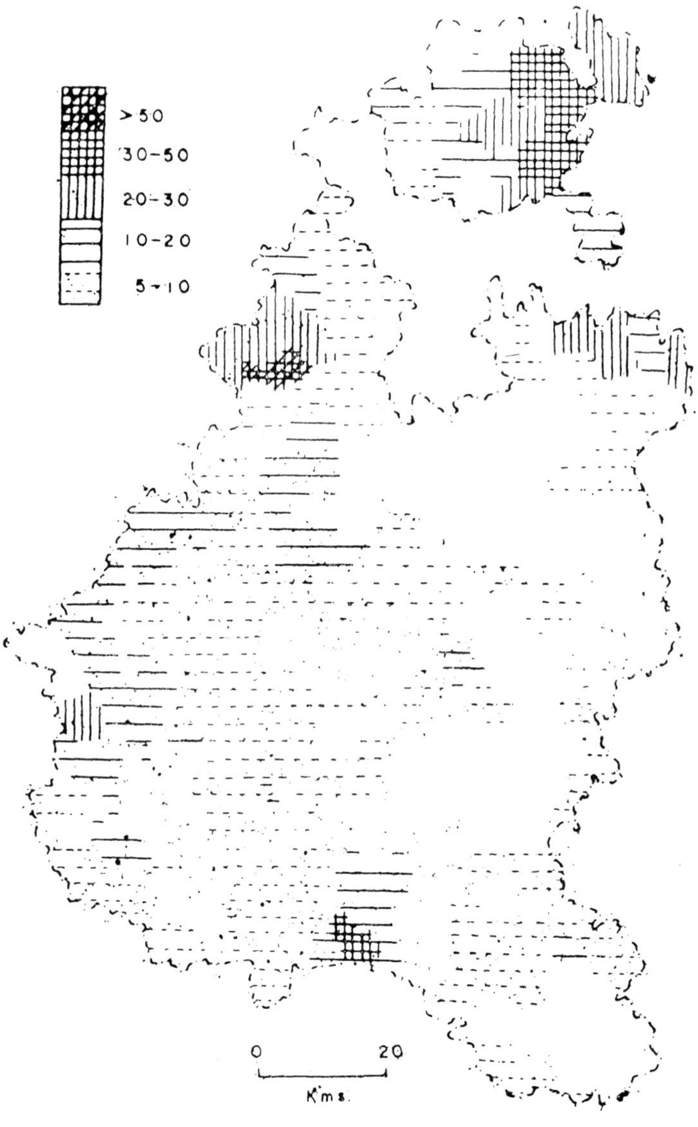

FIG. 3.4

band of low to medium acreage under jowar running north-south is clearly seen (Fig 3.4). Except for a single cluster in Pavagada taluk and another in Sira taluk, it is not a dominant crop in any part of the district.

Intervillage differences in acreage under jowar for the sample clusters are given in Table 3.7

TABLE 3.7

Intervillage variations in per cent area under Jowar

No. of villages in the sample clusters	% area under Jowar	% Coefficient of variation
137	< 5	103
97	5-10	97
37	10-20	62
5	20-30	24
14	30-50	48

Since the number of villages in the sample cluster with acreage of jowar above 20 per cent are only 2 the coefficients of variation are not strictly comparable to see any trend in them. However, in other three classes, the variations within the clusters are higher in areas where the acreage is very low. Such a pattern is similar to those of ragi and rice discussed earlier.

Minor millets are characterised by similar physical requirements as jowar. In addition the various types of minor millets grow in drought as well as water logged area. In Tumkur district they are raised wholly as dry land crop on poor soils.

Minor millets are mainly concentrated in Sira taluk (Fig. 3.5), wherein a large number of clusters record over 30 per cent of the area devoted to major crops. Bordering this millet core is the medium concentration clusters in northern Madhugiri and low proportions of acreage in C.N. Halli and Tiptur. Some clusters in Pavagada also record medium to high proportions of acreage under this crop. About 150 clusters record millet acreage of less than 5 per cent including 6 clusters where millet is not raised at all. Only 4 clusters show millet acreage of about 20 per cent.

Area under Minor Millets as per cent of Area under Major Crops

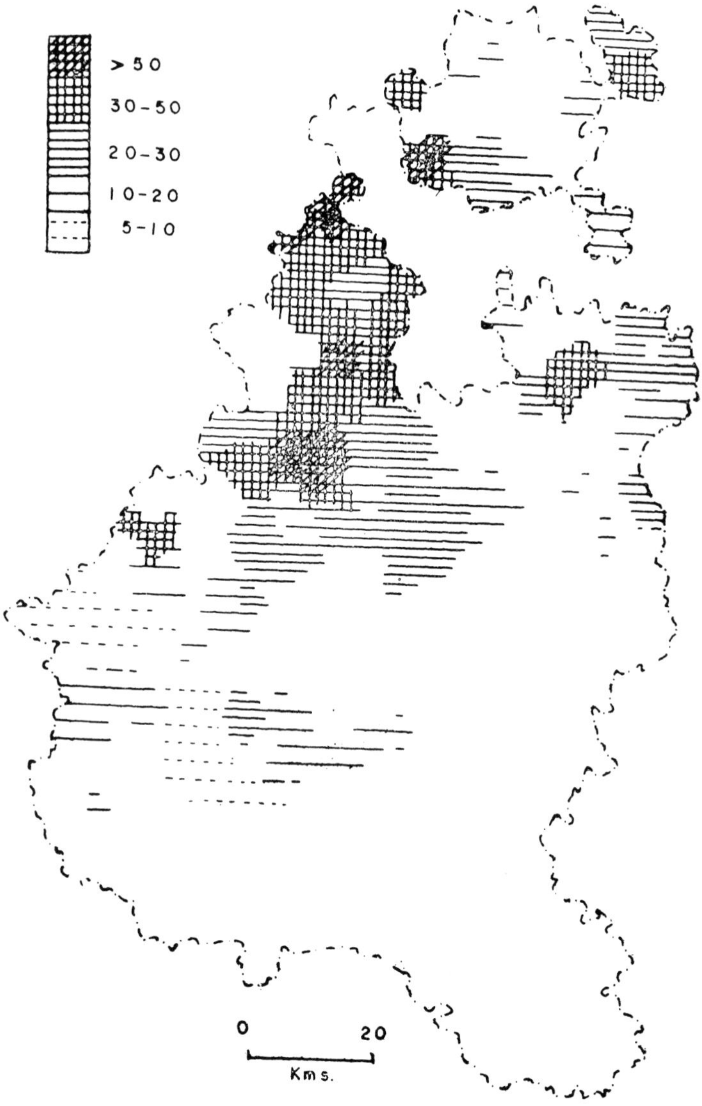

FIG. 3.5

As in the case of other crops, wherever the proportion of area under minor millets is high, intervillage variations are less as compared to areas where minor millets are relatively unimportant as indicated by Table 3.8.

TABLE 3.8

Intervillage variations in per cent area under minor millets

No. of villages in the sample clusters	% area under minor millets	% Coefficient of variation
146	< 5	171
75	5-10	123
34	10-20	105
5	20-30	98
14	30-50	68

However, since the area under minor millets is very small and highly localised in the district the intervillage variation is generally much higher as compared to the crops discussed earlier.

Oilseeds in most cases are rotated with ragi, particularly castor. However, in the Tumkur district groundnut is of significance on its own as a crop. It is essentially a dry land crop, but restricted to better class of soils. Groundnut records considerable proportion in many taluks of the district. Groundnut is also of value as a rotation crop since its cultivation can improve the fertility of the soil. It can be successfully cultivated in areas with rainfall below 20″ and also as high as 50″. It is not however drought resistant and cannot stand water logging.

Castor is tolerant to drought and grows well in relatively dry warm regions with well distributed rainfall of 20 to 30 . All types of soils suit the crop but red sandy loam is used for raising castor in Tumkur district as in other parts of southern India. Much of the inferior soils not fit for commercial and food crops are used for castor. In Tumkur district it is largely mixed with ragi, pulses and other oilseeds like gingilee. Two varieties of castor, one suited for black soils in the northern taluks and the other southern parts suitable for red soil are to be found in the district.

The spatial pattern of distribution mapped in Fig. 3.6 clearly brings out the concentration of acreage in the clusters of

Area under Oilseeds as per cent of Area under Major Crops

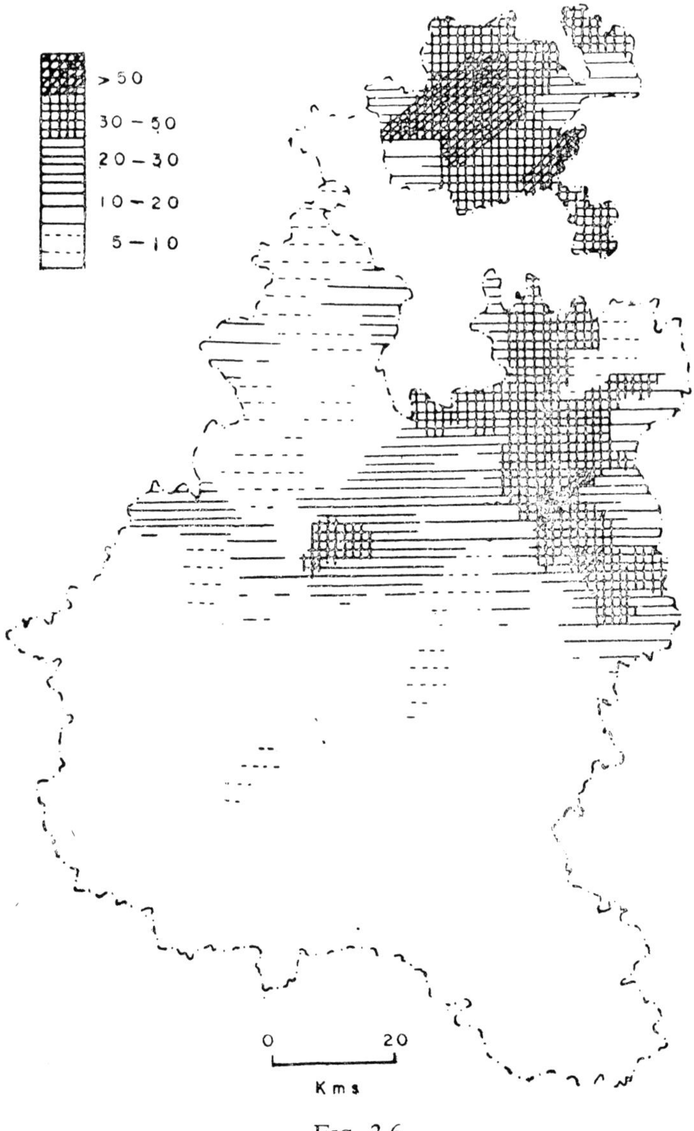

FIG. 3.6

northern taluks of Pavagada, Sira, Madhugiri and Koratgere and its conspicuous absence in the southern parts. However, we must realise that since castor, sesamum and gingilee are more often than not mixed with ragi as mentioned earlier, they do not stand out as independent crops in these parts. Thus, what the pattern on the map brings out largely is the concentration of groundnuts in the four taluks mentioned above. As can be seen, of the four taluks, Sira indicates concentration of medium proportions in oilseed acreage as compared to the other three taluks.

Only seven of clusters do not report areas under oilseeds, whereas 104 clusters record less than 5 per cent area. Twenty-three clusters record between 30-50 per cent area under oilseeds. Among the eight clusters that record over 50 per cent under oilseeds, six are located in Pavagada taluk.

Many of the clusters that record proportions below 5 per cent are located all over the district, but much of them would be oilseeds like sesamum, gingilee and castor.

Intervillage variations follow similar pattern as in other crops (Table 3.9), i.e., core areas show lesser intervillage variations in acreage within clusters than areas which are devoted marginally to these crops.

TABLE 3.9

Intervillage variations in per cent area under Oilseeds

No. of villages in the sample clusters	Percentage area under oilseeds	% Coefficient of variation
133	< 5	117
42	5-10	57
21	10-20	74
29	20-30	96
46	30-50	38

Tur (*togari*) a widely planted pulse in the district is mixed with ragi. Being deep rooted it breaks up the sub-soil and thus renovates it. As long as the soil is not deficient in lime it can be grown on any type of soil. Well drained light to medium soils that permit easy development of roots suit the crop best. It is not a dominant crop in any part of the district, as elsewhere in India. Being one of the mixed crops along with ragi, jowar, etc.,

Area under Tur as per cent of Area under Major Crops

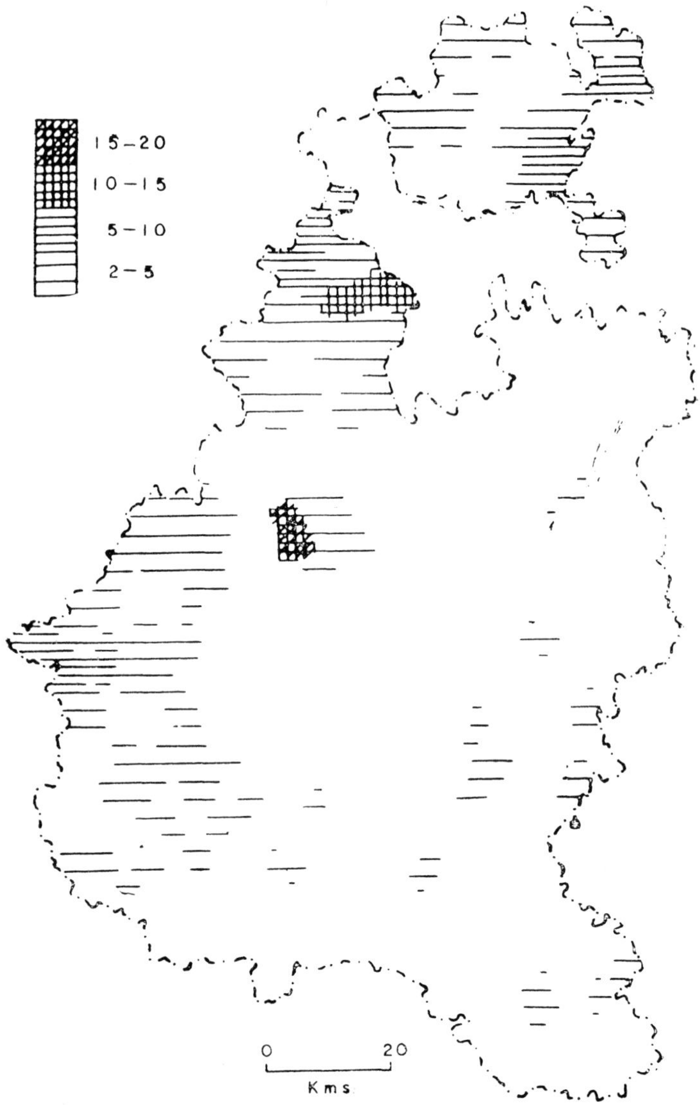

FIG. 3.7

tur is universally planted in rows interspersed with the major crops.

It occupies a minor part of the major crops, consequently many of the clusters record 2—5 per cent area under tur-concentrated mainly in the western parts of Tiptur, C.N. Halli, Sira and a large part of Pavagada taluks. No where the area exceeds an acreage of 15 per cent except for two clusters in Sira and one in C.N. Halli (Fig. 3.7).

Since it is normally mixed with other major foodgrains, over 150 clusters record percentage acreage up to 2 (not shown in the map). Only 10 of the clusters record more than 5 per cent area under tur. Intra-cluster variation is very high in areas which have less than 2 per cent acreage under the crop (197 per cent) as against villages in clusters that record 2—5 per cent area with 74 per cent coefficient of variation.

Sugarcane one of the important cash crops is raised in many parts of the district to some extent except C.N. Halli and Tiptur. Sugarcane grows best on medium heavy soils and under conditions of heavy irrigation on light soils. In Tumkur district as in other parts of southern India, it is grown on reddish loam and black soils. Rainfall between 14″-48″ suits the cultivation of sugarcane. Since the district in general is dry, fibrous varieties are grown.

Although over 200 clusters report some area under sugar-cane cultivation, less than 10 clusters record proportion over 5 per cent acreage. Areas under sugarcane that record over 2 per cent of the area under major crops are shown in Fig. 3.8. The highly restricted parts of sugarcane cultivation is apparent. Two pockets, one covering eastern parts of Madhugiri and Koratgere taluks (the more important of the two), and a minor pocket in Kunigal taluk are to be noticed.

Only 15 of the 32 sample clusters that are being analysed to bring intra-cluster variation recorded some area under sugar-cane. Of these 15, only 2 clusters report between 5-10 per cent area and the rest under 2 per cent. The coefficient of variation for these two clusters are 68 per cent and 86 per cent whereas those 13 clusters that record less than 2 per cent area under sugarcane show an internal variation to the extent of over 200 per cent.

Area under Sugarcane as per cent of Area under Major Crops

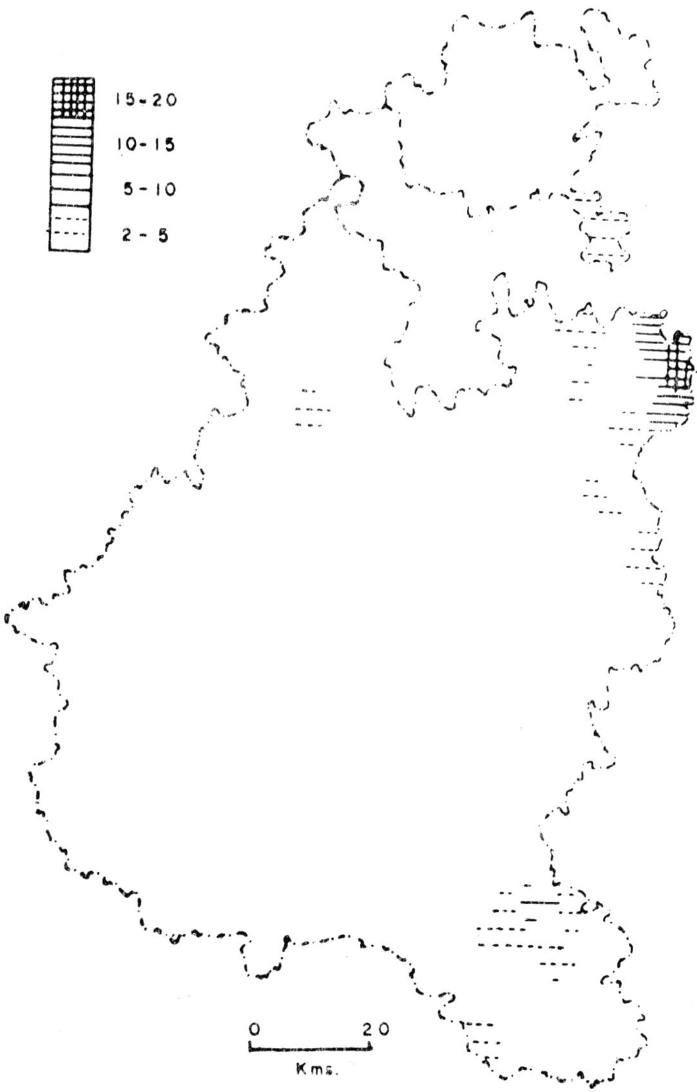

FIG. 3.8

Area under Cotton as per cent of Area under Major Crops

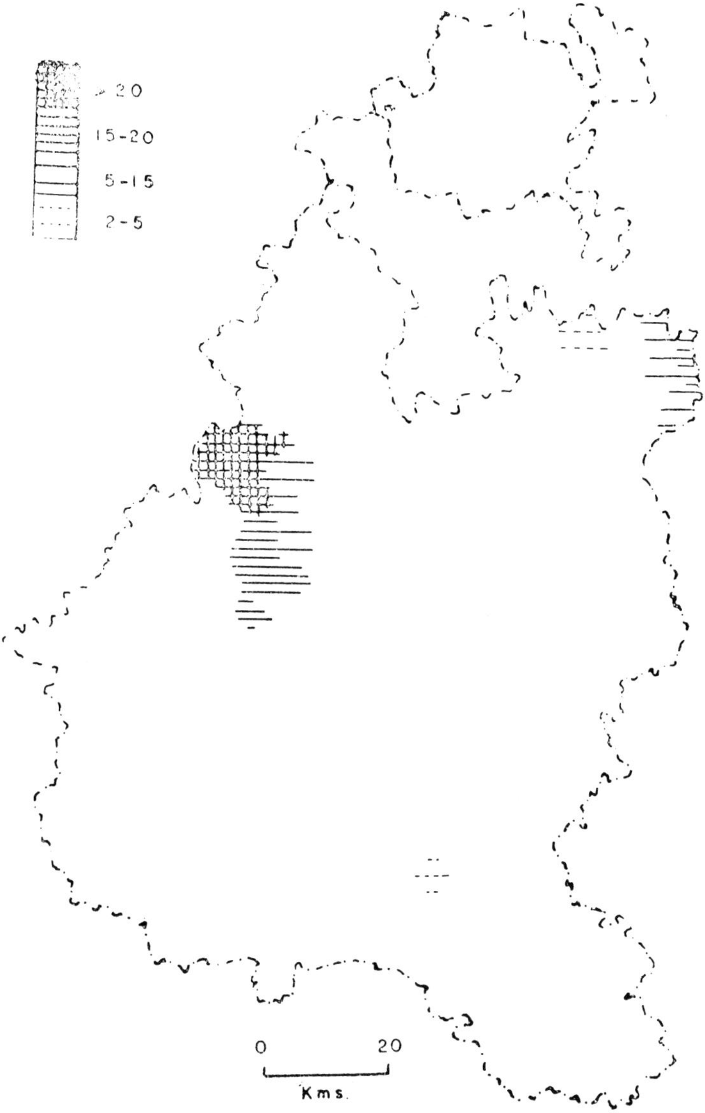

FIG. 3.9

Cotton as a crop occupies insignificant acreage accounting only for 0.24 per cent of the net sown area in the district. Only 50 clusters report area under cotton. Of these over 30 clusters record less than 2 per cent area (not shown in the map). Of the rest cotton concentration is to be found in two patches, a major one in southern Sira and northern C.N. Halli and the other in Madhugiri taluk (Fig. 3.9).

Crop Combinations

The spatial distribution of crops discussed above with the help of a series of maps and tables brings out areas that are important for different crops. The other side of this question is "What are the crops that are important for the various unit areas"? We approach this question by identifying the dominant crop combinations in different clusters following Weaver.[2] A simple method to bring out combination of crops that have significant proportions in the total cropped area has been evolved by Weaver. He compares the actual percentage share of acreage under a crop with an hypothetical percentage. For example, in mono crop area the theoretical percentage share is 100. For a region with two crop combination it is 50 per cent for each, for a crop region it is 33.33, and so on. The deviations from these theoretical norm (100 per cent) with the most dominant crop in a unit area, the deviations of the first two dominant crops with the norm (50, 50), etc., is computed. Whichever combination gives the least deviations form the norm is the crop combination for that unit area. Symbolically,

$$\sigma 2 = \frac{(X_i - \overline{X})^2}{N}$$

where $\overline{X}$ is theoretic norm (100), (50), (33.33), (25), etc., X_i is the actual acreage under the crop. N is the number of crops in the combination. Refinements of this simple method are also available,[3] however, not with marked differences in results.

Crop combinations based on Weaver's method worked out for the various village clusters of the district are mapped in Fig. 3.10. Of the 277 clusters, 97 clusters indicate single crop dominance. Of these 97 except 3 clusters—one where millet is dominant (Sira taluk) and two where oilseeds are dominant (Pavagada taluk)—ragi is the dominant crop. 129 clusters reveal two-crop combinations. These are distributed over 12

Crop Combinations : Rg-Ragi, R-Rice, J-Jowar O-Oilseeds, C-Cotton, M-Minor Millets

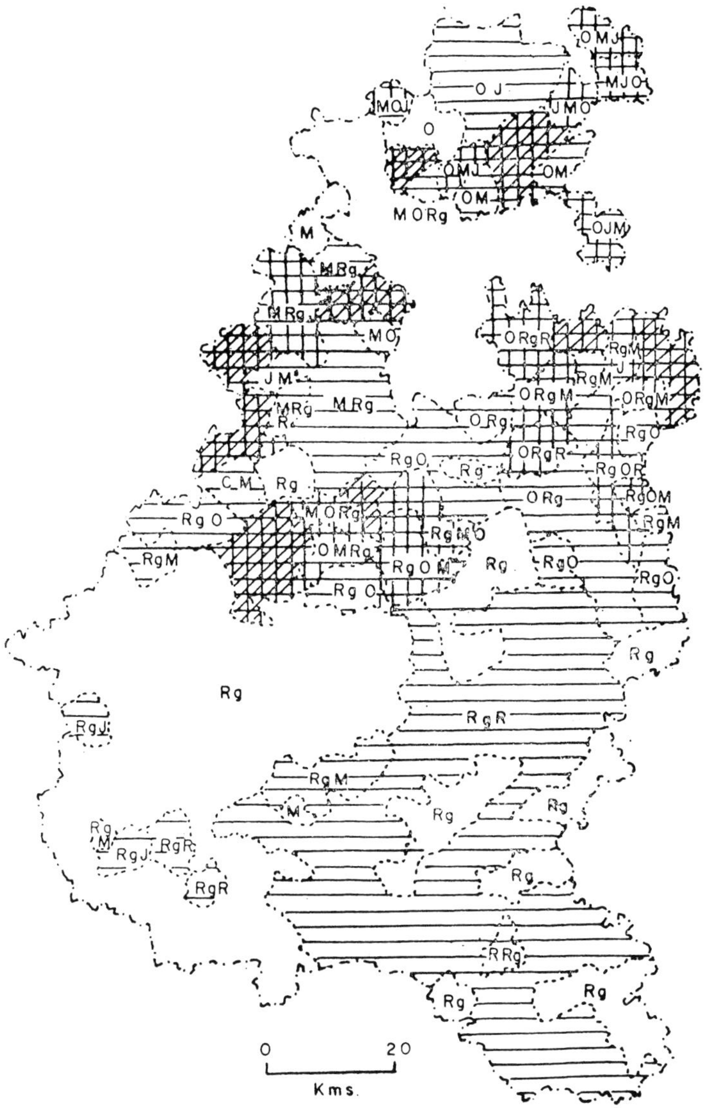

FIG. 3.10

different combinations of crops. The most frequent combination of two crop dominance is ragi and rice (Fig. 3.10)—largely encountered in the taluks of Turuvekere, Kunigal, Tumkur and parts of Gubbi. Ragi and oilseed combinations (13 clusters) are concentrated in parts of Koratgere, Madhugiri and C.N. Halli. An equal number of 13 clusters also indicate oilseed and ragi combination (i.e., oilseed recording larger acreage than ragi). This combination of crop is restricted to parts of Koratgere, Madhugiri and Tumkur taluks.

Oilseed and jowar combinations are recorded by 8 clusters, all restricted to Pavagada taluk. Ragi and millet combination is found in 7 clusters located in the northern parts of Turuvekere and one in C.N. Halli taluk. Millet and ragi in three clusters of Sira and one cluster each with millet and oilseeds, oilseed and millet, jowar and millet, ragi and jowar, and cotton and millet in various parts of the northern taluks, and one cluster with rice dominant followed by ragi as second dominant crop is found in Kunigal taluk.

Three crop combinations are found in about 33 clusters. 15 types of combinations are noticed—the most frequent being oilseeds, ragi and rice. Even in the three-crop combinations, four clusters show the most dominant crop as ragi. It is not surprising to find the occurrence of three-crop combinations in the northern parts of the taluk, since the rainfall/irrigation conditions are poor and the risk of crop failure is taken care of by larger number of crops that are raised. This is also true of the multi-crop cultivation which occur in 19 clusters all situated in the three northern taluks.

Structural Attributes of Agriculture

Spatial aspects of agricultural base have been dealt with in some details in the foregoing sections. It is necessary to probe into the some equally or at times more important structural features of the districts agricultural economy. For this, we depend on the village level data collected from 245 sample villages in the district (Fig. 3.11). Of these 16 village questionnaires are being left out for reasons of incomplete information. Although a large number of facets of the rural society and economy have been collected, we analyse only a part of these information that have direct bearing on the theme of the present study.

Distribution of Sample Villages

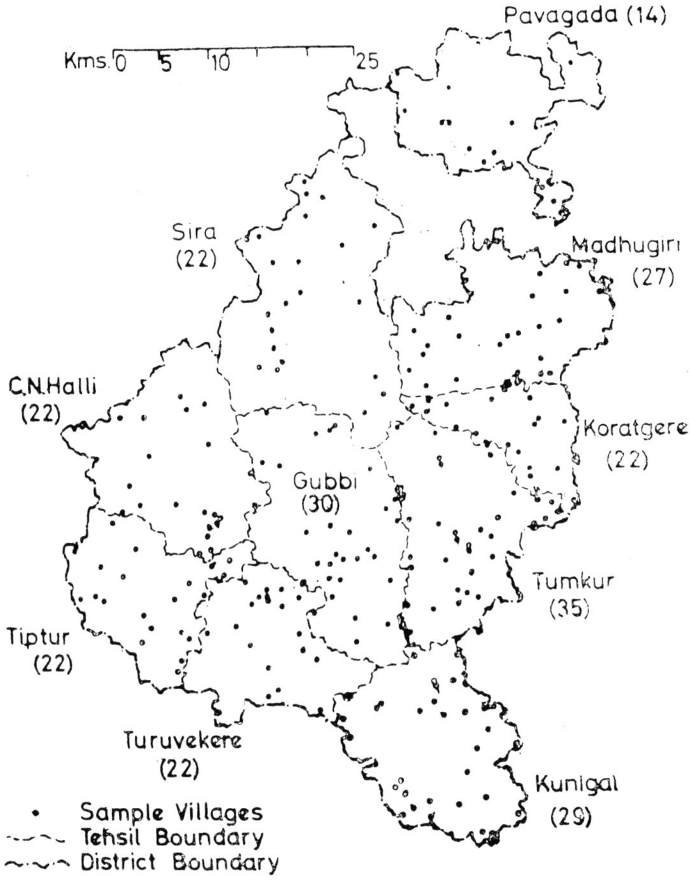

FIG. 3.11

Let us start with the workers in various livelihood categories. The most interesting feature is the increase in the proportion of workers in the agricultural sector (in eight of the taluks, (Table 3.10). Occupations allied to agriculture, however, present a slightly healthy picture with seven of the ten taluks showing an increase in the proportions of workers between 1961 and 1971. Proportion of workers in mining and quarrying has not recorded any change in between 1961 and 1971.

TABLE 3.10

Percentage of male workers to total male workers in primary sector (1961-71)*

Sl. No.	Taluks	Agriculture**		Allied to Agriculture***	
		1961	1971	1961	1971
1.	C.N. Halli	91.5	75.7	12.5	10.2
2.	Gubbi	87.7	94.9	1.8	0.6
3.	Koratgere	75.3	85.7	0.5	1.2
4.	Kunigal	88.0	90.4	1.0	2.8
5.	Madhugiri	86.0	83.6	0.8	5.7
6.	Pavagada	75.1	80.2	1.7	5.8
7.	Sira	79.1	75.4	1.4	6.8
8.	Tiptur	65.7	81.1	16.8	6.1
9.	Tumkur	84.7	74.7	1.2	2.0
10.	Turuvekere	85.4	83.2	4.9	7.2
11.	District	80.0	81.9	3.6	4.7

* Based on 245 sample village data.
** Includes census classification of workers in category I and II.
*** Includes census classification of workers in category III.

The process of increasing proletarianisation in the agricultural sector has been brought out by the fact that percentage point of cultivators decreasing to the tune of 6.20 between two ends of the decade 1961-1971, whereas during the same period agricultural labourers increasing by 8.10 point.[4]

The agricultural census records the distribution of number of operational holdings and the area operated by them (Table 3.11).

TABLE 3.11

Distribution of cultivators and size of holdings (1970-71)

Size of holding (in hectares)	No. of holding	Area operated
0—1	1,20,644 (42%)	53,593 (10%)
1—2	72,530 (25%)	1,05,204 (17%)
2—4	53,497 (19%)	1,48,546 (24%)
4—10	30,807 (11%)	1,80,829 (29%)
Above 10	7,402 (3%)	1,20,350 (20%)
Total	2,85,330 (100%)	6,13,522 (100%)

Small farmers with less than 2 hectares account for about 67 per cent of the holding but operate only 27 per cent of the area. On the other hand the big farmers whose holdings are above 10 hectares constitute only 3 per cent of the cultivators but operate 20 per cent of the area.

Apparently the larger the size of holding larger is the proportion land utilised for non-food crops and vice-versa (Table 3.12). We may notice that the small and medium farmers devote larger proportion of their land to foodgrains than the big farmers. This is the true for practically all the cereals. However, crops like pulses indicate increasing proportions with increasing size of holdings. We also notice a similar trend in the case of jowar and minor millets, however the two together occupy very small proportion of the cropped area, and are highly restricted in their spatial distribution as brought out earlier.

TABLE 3.12

Cropping pattern by size of holdings

Size of holding (in hectares)	Rice	Ragi	Jowar	Minor millets	Pulses	Total food-grains	Ground-nut	Total non-foodgrains
				(Percentage)				
0--1	16.95	39.83	3.80	2.72	13.88	81.94	4.22	18.07
1—2	8.03	38 09	4.45	5 33	19.76	82.96	5.96	17.05
2—4	6.88	35.53	4.60	5.72	19.26	80.06	7.00	19.95
4—10	6.31	29.84	5.80	6 96	18.77	76.78	8.78	23.22
Above 10	5.60	18.94	9 91	8.81	19.94	73.88	12.56	26.12

Source : Based on sample village questionnaires.

This pattern also holds good when we consider the taluk level data (Table 3.13).

Two taluks show a different pattern wherein foodgrains show higher proportion in holdings above 10 hectares as compared to categories of small holdings. The two taluks are Kunigal and Tumkur taluks, where foodgrains in general dominate because of higher proportion of irrigated land and the big farmers continuing to grow rice as brought out in the following pages. We may also notice the differences in dominance of foodcrops across taluks. Food-grain acreage in general is smaller in taluks like C.N. Halli, Gubbi, Koratgere. In spite of this, it is found that big farmers devote a larger proportion of their holdings to non-food commercial crops as compared to small farmers.

TABLE 3.13

Percentage of foodgrain and non-foodgrain crops by size of holdings

Size of holdings Taluk		0—1	1—2	2—10	10 and above
C.N. Halli	(a)	70.05	76.76	74.73	64.19
	(b)	29.95	23.34	25.27	35.81
Gubbi	(a)	71.50	74.00	77.09	63.55
	(b)	28.50	26.00	22.91	36.45
Koratgere	(a)	73.60	69.53	67.05	66.46
	(b)	26.41	30.33	33.56	33.54
Kunigal	(a)	91.33	92.64	93.58	95.62
	(b)	6.25	5.47	4.30	4.38
Madhugiri	(a)	81.39	79.09	80.69	88.20
	(b)	16.88	18.33	16.40	11.61
Pavagada	(a)	78.26	64.64	58.34	62.67
	(b)	21.74	35.36	41.66	37.33
Sira	(a)	83.52	87.76	86.16	86.87
	(b)	16.48	12.24	13.84	13.13
Tiptur	(a)	70.10	71.21	64 77	61.14
	(b)	29.90	28.68	35.12	38.86
Tumkur	(a)	84.72	89.72	88.14	88.50
	(b)	11.79	10.51	11.58	11.50
Turuvekere	(a)	77.92	79.64	70.61	67.57
	(b)	17.98	16.57	23.97	23.65

Source : Based on sample village questionnaires.
(a) Foodgrains (b) Non-Foodgrains

Changes in Cropping Pattern

Based on the sample village data the proportion of acreage under major crops in 1970-71 and 1975-76 are tabulated in Table 3.14.

The crops which have shown increase in percentage area are rice and oilseeds and (a slight increase in) sugarcane. The rest of the crops including ragi register a decrease in percentage acreage devoted to them in the five years. However, no appreciable change in cropping pattern is seen in the district, since a very few crops have shifted their ranks with tur, other pulses, losing their ranks by one place and sugarcane and oilseeds gaining by one.

TABLE 3.14

Change in cropping pattern in the sample villages of the district

Crops	% area to gross cropped area	
	1970-71	1975-76
Paddy	10.98	12.13
Ragi	30.87	29.23
Jowar	6.26	5.92
Tur	1.08	0.97
Other pulses	16.77	15.53
Groundnut	10.89	9.12
Other oilseeds	12.87	16.55
Cotton	0.54	0.36
Sugarcane	0.86	1.00
Coconut	5.20	4.98

Source : Based on sample village questionnaires.

High yielding and improved varieties of crops were introduced in the State on a large scale from about mid-sixties. By 1970-71 the per cent area under HYV to gross cropped area in the district recorded 13.5 per cent and it increased to 16.2 per cent by 1975-76. Among the various crops under HYV in 1976-77, ragi accounts for about 50 per cent followed by paddy (19 per cent) and groundnut (15 per cent). Although the proportion of area under HYV has been fluctuating between 1970-71 and 1976-77 with reference to various crops and over the ten taluks, the general crop domination under HYV has been ragi, rice and groundnut.

However, between this period, crops like ragi and jowar have registered an appreciable increase in the yield (Table 3.15). On the other hand a number of crops including paddy, groundnut, pulses and oilseeds have recorded a decline in their yield, corresponding figures for number of farmers growing these crops and area under these crops are also recorded in the table.

A study of these figures reveal the number of farmers growing ragi have increased, whereas area under ragi has declined indicating the farmers with smaller holdings are increasingly adopting high yielding varieties of ragi, explained largely by the increasing yields of the crop. A reversal of this

TABLE 3.15

Adoption and growth of HYV crops

Crops	No. of farmers growing the crop		Area		Yield per acre	
	1970-71	1975-76	1970-71	1975-76	1970-71	1975-76
Ragi	3826	3903	8093	7312	4.38	5.88
Paddy	2285	1826	2706	2837	20.19	16.25
Maize	432	468	743	645	14.85	11.52
Jowar	371	514	473	407	7.58	8.20
Wheat	115	185	122	102	9.11	9.70
Groundnut	678	623	1926	2263	3.60	2.43
Pulses	187	547	719	809	2.5	2.02
Other oilseeds	195	363	131	393	3.73	1.82

Source : Based on sample village questionnaires.

relationship is to be noticed in the case of paddy where the number of farmers growing the crop decreased and the area increased, indicating only big farmers are concentrating on high yielding varieties of paddy despite to decreasing yields. This is also true of groundnut. However, in the case of pulses and oilseeds despite considerable increase in the number of farmers adopting HYV crops, the area has not registered corresponding growth. This indicates that small farmers are taking to high yielding varieties in pulses and oilseeds despite decrease in their yields. This is made possible since the two crops are usually mixed crops as we have seen earlier and it does help the small farmers in getting cash for their products.

Secondary and Tertiary Sectors

Since the non-agricultural sector of the economy is not rooted to the land but activity and worker based much of our analysis of the secondary and tertiary sector will be based on data relating to types of activities and proportion of workers engaged in them. Among the rural workers in the district about 5 per cent are engaged in secondary activities of household and non-household character as per 1971 census. We have already indicated about the small proportion of income generated by the industrial sector which has shown a constantly declining trend between 1960-61, 1970-71 and 1975-76 with corresponding contribution of 11.2 per cent, 8.6 per cent and 5.7 per cent of the district's income. Large scale establishment in the district is represented by the cement factory at Ammasandra that employs 900 workers. There are 600 registered factories in the small scale sector accounting for an employment of 2900 persons. Traditional handicrafts industries in the form of 17,173 establishments employing about 47,000 people are also scattered throughout the district.

Livelihood of the Workers

An excellent analysis of workers in industrial group on the basis of census data pertaining to the district for 1961 and 1971 is available elsewhere and as such it is unwarranted to repeat the exercise here.[5] With the changing definitions, and other associated problems of data on workers, we may be better off in considering the male workers in various activities in the secondary and tertiary sectors.

The proportion of workers engaged in different livelihood categories are recorded for male workers for the various taluks and the district in Table 3.16. Let us look at the household industry which is the initial form of diversification of rural activities. The absolute number of workers as well as the proportion have registered considerable decrease in the district between 1961 and 1971. This trend holds individually for the taluks. Obviously, it is not a desirable trend. However, the number of rural male workers has increased in the non-primary sector between the same period from 3.9 lakhs to 4.2 lakhs. Manufacturing activity in the non-household industry has at the same time shown an increase. Except Tiptur taluk the absolute number of workers have increased during the period in non-household manufacturing activity. Although there is an overall increase in construction activities in the district indicated by workers in them as well as their proportions to the total workers, there are taluks where both absolute and proportions have decreased during the decade (Table 3.16). Tertiary sector (including occupational categories, VII, VIII and IX) have increased considerably. Of the three categories included, workers engaged in services have decreased and workers in other two categories have shown increase much more than the productive sector (categories Va and Vb). This pattern is also consistent for all the taluks. This tertiarisation of the district's

TABLE 3.16

Rural male workers in non-primary activities : (1961 and 1971)

Sl. No.	Taluks		Household Industry	Non-household Industry	Construction activities	Trade and Commerce	Transport, storage and communication	Other services	Total workers (including primary workers)
1.	C.N. Halli	(a)	1808(5.38)	342(1.02)	368(1.10)	465(1.39)	66(0.20)	1575(4.68)	33651
		(b)	1120(2.92)	495(1.25)	556(1.45)	764(2.51)	132(0.35)	1267(3.30)	38537
2.	Gubbi	(a)	2765(6.28)	244(0.56)	195(0.45)	373(0.85)	70(0.16)	1325(3.01)	44032
		(b)	1191(2.63)	465(1.01)	110(0.25)	540(1.19)	234(0.52)	1345(2.97)	45361
3.	Koratgere	(a)	1918(6.79)	200(0.71)	101(0.36)	484(1.72)	29(0.11)	1368(4.85)	28246
		(b)	513(1.76)	247(0.35)	174(0.60)	513(1.76)	58(0.20)	963(3.29)	29270
4.	Kunigal	(a)	1834(4.11)	290(0.65)	162(0.37)	417(0.94)	52(0.12)	1549(3.47)	44662
		(b)	873(1.85)	250(0.75)	172(0.37)	755(1.60)	154(0.33)	1439(3.05)	47225
5.	Madhugiri	(a)	4307(9.07)	281(0.60)	274(0.58)	880(1.86)	45(0.10)	2312(4.87)	47491
		(b)	1242(2.37)	516(0.99)	445(0.85)	1069(2.04)	116(0.22)	2006(3.82)	52585
6.	Pavagada	(a)	5076(14.61)	303(0.88)	482(1.39)	766(2.21)	26(0.08)	2057(5.92)	34745
		(b)	1778(4.52)	350(0.89)	509(1.30)	905(2.3)	93(0.24)	1358(3.45)	39370
7.	Sira	(a)	3774(8.42)	289(0.65)	272(0.61)	528(1.18)	35(0.08)	2227(4.97)	44487
		(b)	2189(4.75)	569(1.24)	437(0.95)	776(1.69)	94(0.21)	1842(3.99)	46155

8. Tiptur	(a)	2522(8.06)	418(1.34)	330(1.19)	433(1.39)	38(0.13)	1397(4.46)	31317
	(b)	1402(4.07)	273(0.80)	324(0.94)	756(2.19)	169(0.49)	1277(3.70)	34507
9. Tumkur	(a)	2324(4.43)	758(1.45)	396(0.76)	851(1.63)	184(0.35)	2944(5.62)	52449
	(b)	986(1.82)	1061(1.95)	723(1.33)	1265(2.33)	501(0.92)	3203(5.89)	5444
10. Turuvekere	(a)	1911(6.26)	315(1.04)	104(0.34)	278(0.91)	60(0.20)	969(3.78)	30549
	(b)	802(2.38)	892(2.65)	272(0.81)	639(1.90)	264(0.79)	1300(3.86)	33711
11. District total	(a)	28239(7.21)	3440(0.88)	2724(0.70)	5475(1.40)	605(0.16)	16723(4.27)	391989
	(b)	12096(2.88)	5218(0.89)	3722(0.81)	8187(1.95)	1815(0.43)	16000(3.80)	421135

Note : (a) refers to 1961 data.

(b) refers to 1971 data.

Figures in parentheses are percentage to total workers in the taluks.

rural economy without a strong secondary setcor is a typical character of underdeveloped areas. This phenomena is also true for urban areas in the district where much of the urban workers are engaged in tertiary sector as compared to the secondary sector and consequently the towns are referred to as service towns in most cases.

Composition of Industrial Activities

Let us now turn from workers engaged in these activities to the structure of the activities included in these sectors. In addition to the large scale industry producing cement located at Ammasandra (Turuvekere taluk), there are 600 registered small scale industries of which a little over 60 per cent employ more than 5 persons. The structure of these industries is brought out in Table 3.17, which gives proportions of units employing more than 30 persons in the district in different types of industries.

TABLE 3.17

Percentage of small scale industries employing more than 30 persons

Type of Industry	Percentage of units to total units
Mineral based	2.40
Agricultural based	47.31
Forest based	20.36
Consumer based	29.94

Source : Compiled from Techno-Economic Survey Report — Rural Industries Projects by Government of Kanataka, 1974.

Reflecting the character of the agricultural district, over 70 per cent of such units are based on raw materials from primary sources. Besides these, there are over 17,000 small units including traditional and handicraft industries which employ about 47,000 persons. The various types of units are grouped into 5 types of industries and their structure is brought out in the following paragraphs.

Table 3.18 records the percentage of units in the various taluks in the five groups of industries. The most dominant units are based on livestock resources over the activities include farming, wool-weaving and leather stitching. Activities based on these resources are prominant in the northern taluks of Sira, Pavagada and C.N. Halli, which house within them 80 per cent of the establishments in the district. The next important type of industries are those based on raw materials from agricultural sources, like edible oil, cotton and silk looms, flour mills, etc. Apparently four taluks account for 70 per cent of the establishment of this type in the district. Third in strength is the consumer-oriented establishments like bakeries, confectionary, engineering, soap manufacture, etc., which account for about 25 per cent. Obviously, these establishments are more ubiquitously distributed among the various taluks.

TABLE 3.18

Percentage of traditional and handicraft units to the district totals*

Sl. No.	Taluks	Mineral	Agricultural based	Forest	Live-stock based	Consumer based	Others
1.	C.N. Halli	3	7	4	25	5	11
2.	Gubbi	4	27	5	2	7	1
3.	Koratgere	8	2	6	4	15	3
4.	Kunigal	7	5	10	1	17	41
5.	Madhugiri	51	13	34	10	13	3
6.	Pavagada	8	8	7	30	8	18
7.	Sira	4	3	7	25	7	—
8.	Tiptur	2	19	2	2	8	—
9.	Tumkur	6	5	18	2	13	16
10.	Turuvekere	6	11	6	1	7	—

*Values are rounded off to nearest integer.

Secondary activities based on mineral products like bricks and tiles, pottery and those based on forests and trees including saw mills, coir/rope industries etc., account for about 7 per cent each. These establishments are dominant in Madhugiri taluk. These units deal with stone works, limestone burning, brick manufacturers, production of mats and rope.

We may now see what types of industries are important for each taluk (Table 3.19). Since the three northern taluks of Sira, Pavagada and C.N. Halli account for 80 per cent of the industrial units based on livestocks resources, such units are also dominant within these taluks. Gubbi, Turuvekere and Tiptur are dominated by secondary activities based on agricultural raw materials (cotton, silk, edible oils). Koratgere and Kunigal taluks record prominence of units oriented to consumer products. Madhugiri and Tumkur record more diversified secondary activities.

TABLE 3.19

Distribution of types of units in various taluks (percentage to total units in the taluks)*

Sl. No.	Taluks	Mineral based	Agriculture based	Forest based	Livestock based	Consumer based	Others
1.	C.N. Halli	2	16	4	69	8	1
2.	Gubbi	3	71	6	6	12	2
3.	Koratgere	12	8	12	23	45	—
4.	Kunigal	9	21	20	4	45	1
5.	Madhugiri	24	20	23	19	12	3
6.	Pavagada	5	14	6	67	9	—
7.	Sira	3	7	7	70	10	2
8.	Tiptur	2	67	3	8	19	1
9.	Tumkur	7	19	31	10	30	3
10.	Turuvekere	9	54	14	4	20	—

*Values are rounded off to nearest integer.

About 75 per cent of the workers engaged in manufacturing activities are engaged in household industry in the district. Much of the production of textiles, wooden products, leather and leather products, pottery, edible oil extraction are in the household sector.

Spatial Patterns of Workers

We now proceed with an analysis of spatial patterns of the workers in the three livelihood categories of household, non-household manufacturing sector and the tertiary sector (Census category VII and IX).

Clusterwise workers in household industry as a percentage to the total workers (1971) are mapped for the district (Fig. 3.12.). From our analysis of manufacturing activities it is obvious that some of the highly concentrated areas of this

Workers in Household Industry as per cent of all Workers

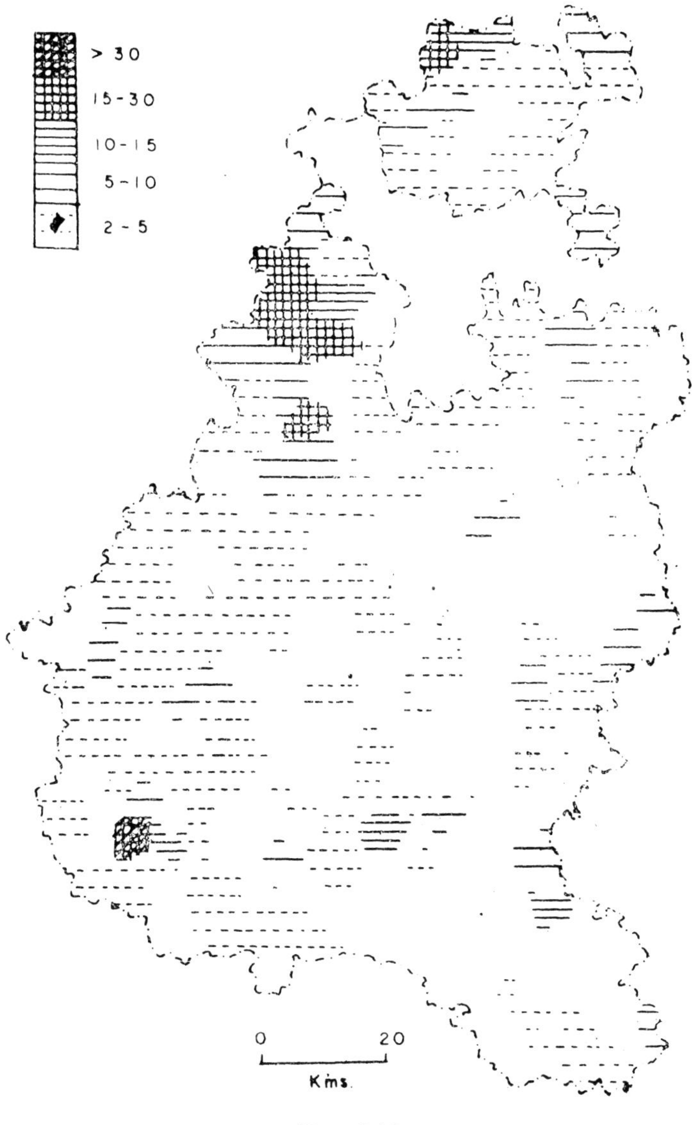

FIG. 3.12

sector are to be encountered in Sira and Pavagada. It can also be seen that areas which indicate higher intensity of cropping usually show lower proportion of manufacturing activity. Only five clusters of 277 clusters do not record workers in household industry. About 140 clusters show workers in this category below 2 per cent, and another 108 clusters between 2—5 per cent. Only 3 clusters show more than 20 per cent workers in household industry. Unlike the crop pattern, which are land-based and hence core areas (which normally occur in contiguous stretches) show lesser intervillage variations than peripheral areas, concentrations of workers in household industry itself occur in small patches and show intracluster variation more in clusters where the activity is found in greater intensity than clusters where the concentration of the industry is less (Table 3.20).

TABLE 3.20

Intervillage variations in per cent workers in household industries

No. of villages in the sample clusters	% workers	% Coefficient of variation
133	< 2	148
91	2–5	101
9	5—10	156
17	10—15	189
8	15+	102

Distribution of manufacturing workers in the non-household industry is much more sparse as seen from Fig. 3.13. Much of the occurrence of this category of workers are within urban influence areas, or located near to urban places. Sixteen clusters do not record any workers in this category, whereas 224 clusters show less than 2 per cent workers, and 30 clusters between 2 and 5 per cent. Only 7 clusters record over 5 per cent workers in non-household industry of which 5 are in the urban influence zones.

Workers in tertiary sector are more ubiquitous—all clusters recording some proportion in this sector. Over 250 clusters record more than 2 per cent. The modal class is between 2-5 per cent (144 clusters). Twenty-three clusters located in various

Workers in Non-household Industry as per cent of all Workers

FIG. 3.13

parts of the districts, as shown in the map, record more than 10 per cent workers in tertiary sector. As in the case of workers in manufacturing activities intervillage variations are large in concentrated areas as compared to clusters where the activity is weak (Table 3.21).

TABLE 3.21

Intervillage variation in per cent workers in tertiary sector

No. of villages in the sample cluster	% Workers	% Coefficient of variation
137	< 5	112
104	5—10	132
33	10—20	156

We may conclude our analysis of the economic base of the district with the following observations. The physical environment of the district favours dry crop cultivation. Although the proportion of irrigated area is likely to increase substantially in parts of the district (Tiptur, Turuvekere, and Gubbi taluks) by the middle of eighties with the completion of Hemavathi Project, since the water is stipulated to be used for dry crops only, we do not foresee any change in the cropping pattern. Agriculture not only remains the major income generating sector but also increasing its proportion of contribution. Correspondingly the direct dependence on agriculture of the workers has also registered an increase. This increase is more pronounced in the labour segment rather than the cultivating segment. With the increasing possibility of irrigation it is necessary to launch a more intensive programme for promoting high yielding varieties of ragi, pulses and oilseeds which have registered higher adoption rate against the small farmer group. The entire northern parts are likely to continue with their dependence on larger number of crops (to offset crop failure). For such areas programmes for augmenting and dispersing edible oil manufacturing facilities as well as industries based on livestock resources (leather products including tanning, woollen looms etc.) is indicated. With a not so happy experience o implanted factories, it may be better to direct the investmen

Workers in Tertiary Activities as per cent of all Workers

FIG. 3.14

on increasing the productivity of the people who are engaged in these activities through improved technology of production of their products.

We have noticed increasing tertiarisation of the rural economy without the necessary development of secondary sector. It is obvious, therefore, that the increasing tertiary sector particularly of trade and commerce both in rural and urban places is based on agricultural produce. Such programmes may also provide a much needed stronger manufacturing sector to the increasing tertiary sector.

REFERENCES

1. V.K.R.V. Rao, *Issues and Problems of Development of Tumkur*, Key-note Address, Workshop on Population Planning and Area Development for South Asia, UNAPD1 and ISEC, Bangalore, 1978.
2. J.C. Weaver, "Crop Combination Region in the Middle West", *Geographical Review*, XLIV, 1954, 123-200.
3. See for example, D. Thomas : *Agriculture in Wales during Napoleonic Wars*, Wales University Press, 1963, and S.N. Raffiullah, "A New Approach to Functional Classification of Towns". *The Geographer*, XII, 1965, 40-53.
4. V.K.R.V. Rao, *Issues and Problems of Development of Tumkur*, Key-note address presented at the Workshop on Population Planning and Area Development for South Asia, Bangalore, 1978, p. 29.
5. P.N. Mari Bhat, "Population, Education and Employment in Tumkur District, 1921-71 : A Census Analysis" (Mimeo), ISEC, Bangalore, 1978.

4

Habitat, Central Functions and Levels of Interaction

HUMAN HABITATS are differentiated by their size and concomitant functional characteristics. However, clear distinction in such attributes is much more marked in urban systems that rest upon the vast rural hinterland rather than rural settlements. The settlement system gets integrated through the surplus produced in the rural hinterland which gets exchanged for the services and products of the urban centres, resulting in a complex pattern of interactions. Size and functional differences result in a hierarchy of settlements in the space economy wherein a few centres with a large number of services and production activities occupy the apex through a larger number of less complex settlements to a much larger set of rural settlements in a pyramidal structure. It is not necessary to labour upon the efficiency and virtues of the hierarchical arrangement of settlements in organising a space economy, since the theme is amply covered in uncountable number of writings. The more crucial part of this hierarchical arrangement is the pattern of links within and between different (hierarchical) orders of settlements. We restrict the use of the hierarchic concept to the tertiary and service functions of settlements.

Since the hierarchic arrangement of settlements is an empirical reality and a product of natural evolution of the settlement system, we begin with the identification of the existing hierarchy and later pass on to estimate the level of intervillage interaction that can be a poser to the strengthening upward links. Much as we wish to utilise the exchange pattern of products of these villages to bring out the process of suction mechanism that we suspect is operating in the space economy, our appetite for data seems much too large for what is available.

Distribution of Central Functions

The location of certain service functions in a settlement increases its centrality and importance. These functions for which people travel from other settlements are what has come to be labelled as central functions. A number of services with their locations are readily available in the census records in the form of infrastructural amenities available to the villages. However, all these are not to be included as central functions. Some of the variables may be relegated so as to sieve out those which are infrastructural but do not attract people from other settlements (e.g., availability of electricity, water, etc.).

Thus, we select the following functions as indicators of centrality of the settlement:

1. Middle School
2. Secondary School
3. Medical Facilities (e.g., Dispensary, Health Centre, Private medical practitioner, etc.)
4. Post Office
5. Telegraph Office
6. Weekly Markets.

All these are not of equal importance in the sense that, some are more numerous and hence attract little movement from other places, while others are fewer in number and attract a large number of people from longer distances. A study of distribution of these functions will reveal the differences in the importance of these functions. Out of the 2452 inhabited villages in the district 1643 villages have primary schools (63 per cent of the villages) and because of this wider incidence of the primary school it has not been included in the analysis. About 22 per cent of the villages house middle schools whereas only about 3 per cent each have secondary school (79), and medical facilities (78). Post offices, telegraph offices and weekly markets are found in 15.83 per cent, 1.23 per cent and 2.49 per cent of the villages respectively.

The distribution of these functions in various taluks are

tabulated in table 4.1. The single important feature is the more or less uniform distribution of functions across the ten taluks. However, the distance between the location of some of these functions and the settlements bring out significant differences between taluks.

TABLE 4.1

Talukwise distribution of central functions

Taluks	Inhabited village	No. of villages with					
		Middle school	Sec. school	Post office	P & T office	Medical facilities	Weekly market
1. C.N. Halli	217	42	9	31	6	6	5
2. Gubbi	296	52	10	54	4	11	8
3. Koratgere	226	32	5	23	2	5	5
4. Kunigal	291	37	8	46	5	9	5
5. Madhugiri	276	39	7	55	5	5	8
6. Pavagada	137	38	6	39	3	7	2
7. Sira	224	53	9	55	3	12	10
8. Tiptur	221	50	7	36	7	7	8
9. Tumkur	353	69	10	49	8	9	6
10. Turuvekere	221	49	8	36	5	7	13
district	2452	461	79	424	48	78	70

Through a series of maps we now bring out the distribution of the functions on the basis of village clusters delimited earlier. This will help us in highlighting spatial gaps in the locations of these functions. About 30 of the clusters do not have middle schools. Of these two thirds are located in the urban shadow area (Table 4.2). On the other extreme there are 4 clusters in which more than 60 per cent of the villages contain middle schools, all of them beyond urban shadow areas. In a large number of clusters, however 10-40 per cent of the villages have secondary schools. The spatial distribution of middle schools is mapped in Fig. 4.1. As seen in the map, there are two clusters (one with 4 villages and the other with 3 villages) that record availability of middle schools in all the villages located in them (Sira taluk). Middle schools are, then, well distributed throughout the district. Consequently no village in the district is beyond 2 miles of this function.

Cluster-wise Distribution of per cent Villages Offering Middle School Education

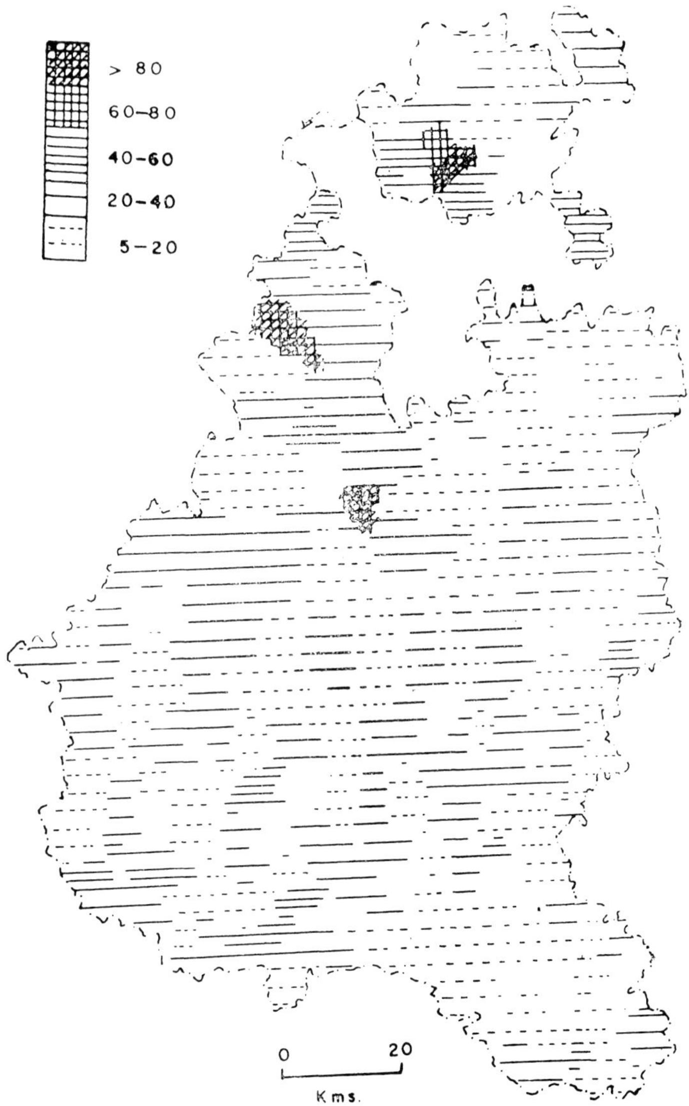

FIG. 4.1

TABLE 4.2

Distribution of clusters by per cent villages with Middle Schools

% villages with Middle schools	In urban shadow		Beyond urban shadow	
	Number	Per cent	Number	Per cent
0	20	23	11	6
10—19.99	27	31	89	47
20—39.99	36	41	76	40
40—59.99	4	5	10	5
60—70.99	—	—	1	—
80+	—	—	3	2
Total	87	100	190	100

TABLE 4.3

Distribution of clusters by per cent villages with post office facility

% of villages with post office facility	Within urban shadow		Beyond urban shadow	
	Number	Per cent	Number	Per cent
0	21	24	12	6
10–20	30	34	96	91
20–40	26	30	68	36
40–60	7	8	11	6
60–80	3	4	2	1
80+	0	0	1	—
Total	87	100	190	100

The number of post offices is only slightly smaller than the strength of the middle schools, resulting in an average of 6 villages per post office. Despite this, 33 clusters record no post office facilities. This is significant since the average size of the clusters is between 6-10 villages. Twenty-one of these 33 clusters are located in the urban shadow areas, and apparently utilise the services offered in the nearest urban centres (Table 4.3). Only one cluster in Sira taluk offers post office facilities in all the three villages in it (Fig. 4.2). These villages are large in population size (the three villages together have a population of over 8000). It is not only that 33 clusters do not have post office facilities, but most of them occur in contiguous patches. Thus, we can see a single contiguous patch of 3 clusters overlapping Madhugiri and Sira taluk boundaries which contain 50 villages that do not record a single post

Cluster-wise Distribution of per cent villages offering Post Office Facilities

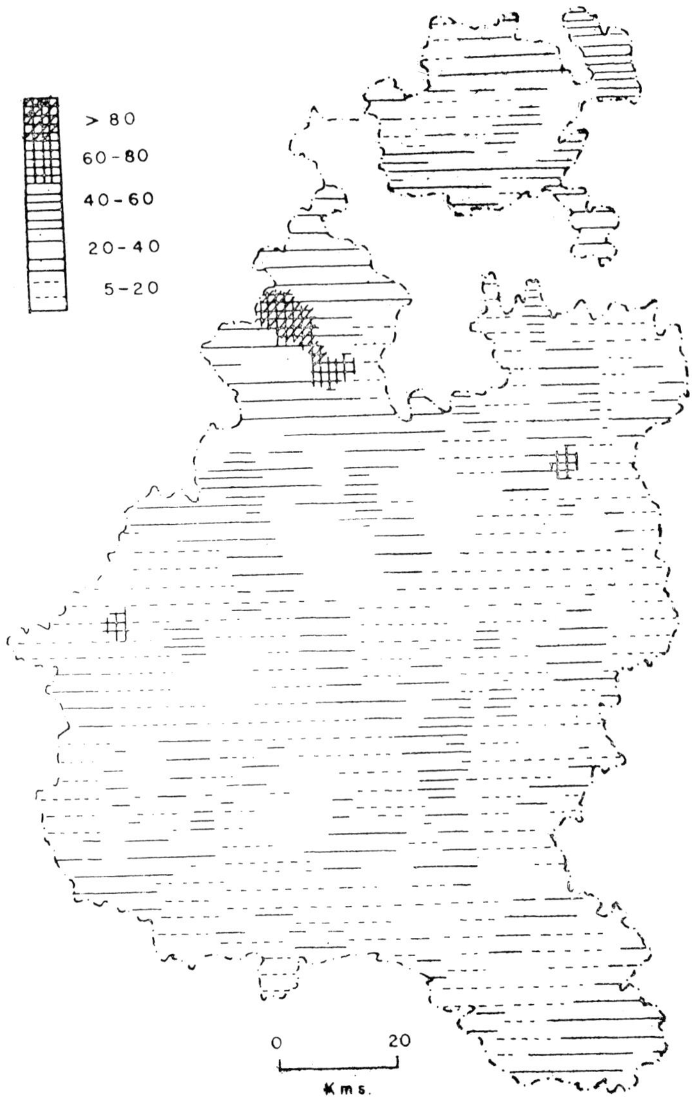

FIG. 4.2

office. Such cases seem to be more frequent within urban shadow areas. On the other hand, within the influence area of Gubbi town, there are 6 post offices in a cluster of 11 villages. Although post offices are well spread out in the district there are areas where locational efficiency is wanting. While the average catchment of the service is 6 villages, it varies from over 20 in some cases to 2 in others. Such a distribution indicates that with a little re-allocation, the reach of this facility can be improved.

Whereas all the villages are within 2 miles reach of a primary school, middle school and post office (in most cases much less than a mile), a considerable number of villages are beyond four miles of a weekly market, secondary school, medical facilities and telegraph office.

In five taluks over 15 per cent of the population lives beyond four miles of secondary school (Table 4.4). Pavagada taluk fares poorly with 31 per cent of its population living beyond four miles of a secondary school. In terms of proportion of villages, C.N. Halli ranks last. In all the taluks, the proportion of villages within 2 miles of this function is smaller than the proportion of population (except Pavagada). This is reversed when a similar comparison is made in the distance range of 2-4 miles. This indicates that not only the population threshold of the location is high but also that the locations are in the midst of large villages.

TABLE 4.4

Distance range in availability of Secondary schools

Sl No.	Taluks	Per cent villages (V) and Population (P) within					
		2 miles		2–4 miles		Beyond 4 miles	
		V	P	V	P	V	P
1.	C.N. Halli	36	52	46	33	18	15
2.	Gubbi	35	46	51	45	14	9
3.	Koratgere	39	33	48	44	13	3
4.	Kunigal	38	40	58	50	14	10
5.	Madhugiri	34	41	52	43	14	16
6.	Pavagada	32	29	53	40	15	31
7.	Sira	37	37	49	34	14	26
8.	Tiptur	45	53	44	32	11	17
9.	Tumkur	31	59	58	34	11	7
10.	Turuvekere	36	50	52	37	12	13

A larger proportion of villages and population are within 2 miles of a secondary school in Tumkur, Tiptur, Koratgere and C.N. Halli taluks. The clusters in which the secondary schools are located are mapped in Fig 4.3. We may notice that several contiguous clusters appear with secondary school locations as well as patches of clusters without the facility. On an average about 31 villages and a population of about 18,000 are expected to be served by a secondary school. Of the 79 vilages that house secondary schools 67 villages have more than 1000 population. Only 8 villages that offer secondary school services have a population size of less than 500. The average distance between the nearest neighbouring secondary school locations is about 7 kilometres, resulting in a range of 3.5 kilometres. Yet, as we have seen earlier a considerable proportion of villages as well as of population live much beyond this range.

In all 76 settlements offer medical services excluding the 12 urban centres. Each centre then is expected to cover 33 villages and a population of about 20,000. Thus the location of this facility assumes greater importance. Only 76 clusters have medical facilities in which two clusters have two villages each offering medical services (Fig. 4.4). A pattern of 'dispersed concentration' is apparent.

In terms of locational efficiency of medical facilities then, Kunigal taluk stands out best with 91 per cent of the villages and 95 per cent of its population within 4 miles of such a facility. In fact 38 per cent of the villages containing 41 per cent of the population of the taluk are within 2 miles (Table 4.5). This is closely followed by Tiptur taluk where 90 per cent of the villages and 95 per cent of its population are within 4 miles of a medical facility and 48 per cent of the villages and 63 per cent of population within a radius of 2 miles. On the other hand, Turuvekere and C.N. Halli taluks have almost 20 per cent of their villages and over 15 per cent of their population beyond 4 miles.

Of the 78 villages that offer medical services, 72 villages have a population size of over 1000 each. The average distance between two nearest medical centres is about 6.6 kilometres. However, as seen above a considerable segment of the society lives beyond the 3·3 kilometre limit.

Distribution of Clusters that offer Secondary Education

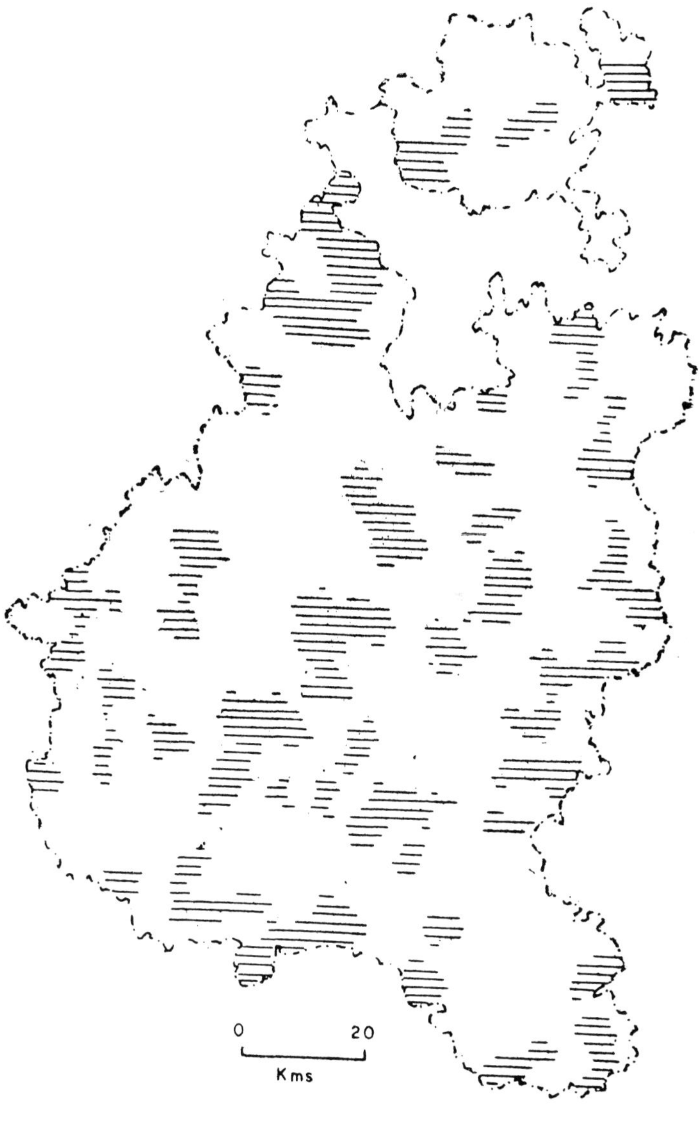

FIG. 4.3

Distribution of Clusters that offer Medical Services (stripes indicate presence of one centre and checks indicate two centres)

FIG. 4.4

TABLE 4.5

Distance range in availability of medical facilities

Sl. No.	Taluks	% villages and population within					
		2 miles		2-4 miles		Beyond 4 miles	
		V	P	V	P	V	P
1.	C.N. Halli	36	45	45	35	19	30
2.	Gubbi	36	50	47	37	17	13
3.	Koratgere	39	51	44	35	17	14
4.	Kunigal	38	47	53	48	9	5
5.	Madhugiri	35	44	53	43	12	87
6.	Pavagada	31	37	53	48	16	15
7.	Sira	36	43	45	44	15	13
8.	Tiptur	48	63	42	32	10	5
9.	Tumkur	31	56	58	37	11	8
10.	Turuvekere	37	52	44	33	19	15

Whereas in some cases 10 contiguous clusters record the presence of medical facilities, there are a large number of continuous patches of clusters where they are absent. It is obvious from the pattern of its location that even with the existing number of health centres, with proper choice of location, a larger number of villages can be brought closer to these facilities.

Telegraph offices are obviously fewer only with 36 villages and 12 urban places offering this service. Thus the average number of villages served by a telegraph office works out to 58 and the population served by it is about 32,800. The locations of the telegraph office show a pattern of dispersed concentration (Fig. 4.5). Such concentrations occur along major transport routes, and near the urban centres. Two patches of four contiguous clusters one in Tumkur taluk and the other in the adjoining Madhugiri taluk are noticed. The rest of the telegraphic offices in the district are spread out but in all cases located near the urban centres.

Two linear arrangements can be seen—one running along Tumkur-Tiptur and the other along Kunigal-Turuvekere routes.

With so few locations of this service a considerable proportion of villages are beyond the 4 miles radius, and in many cases, beyond 8 miles. Apparently the consideration for the location of telegraph offices has been their accessibility to the

Distribution of Clusters that offer Telegraphic Services

FIG. 4.5

urban system and to the telegraphic network system rather than the accessibility of villages to the facility.

Sira and Pavagada are poorly placed with reference to telegraphic facility (more than 65 per cent of these villages and over 50 per cent of this population lying beyond four miles of a telegraph office) as indicated in Table 4.6. Less than 30 villages are located within 2 miles in the two taluks. Tumkur taluk is better off with 27 per cent of its villages and 54 per cent of its population within 2 miles of this service. Since fewer settlements house this facility the distance range is about 5 kilometres as indicated by the average distance between two nearest telegraph offices (10 kilometres).

TABLE 4.6

Distance range in availability of telegraphic service

Sl. No.	Taluks	Per cent villages (V) and population (P) within					
		2 miles		4 miles		beyond 4 miles	
		V	P	V	P	V	P
1.	C.N. Halli	21	31	31	24	48	45
2.	Gubbi	17	25	37	40	46	35
3.	Koratgere	17	25	33	40	50	35
4.	Kunigal	16	25	38	33	46	42
5.	Madhugiri	19	26	30	33	51	51
6.	Pavagada	8	19	26	24	66	57
7.	Sira	6	19	25	30	69	51
8.	Tiptur	19'	36	40	29	41	35
9.	Tumkur	27	54	35	24	38	22
10.	Turuvekere	23	34	37	34	40	32

The location of weekly markets which is essentially based on accumulation of local demands over a period of time, is controlled by an altogether different set of processes than the above discussed functions. These periodic markets which are characteristic of a rural peasant society operate on regularly scheduled days of the week, and not on a permanent basis since per capita demand for goods sold in the market is not large enough to support them. Periodic markets are a business proposition for sellers unlike the functions discussed above where a certain amount of welfare considerations are taken into account. Periodic markets with their virtues of concentrating demand of several market areas in a single place and on specified days are a necessity in serving the inaccessible parts that are removed from the established markets and services of urban places.

Normally, the location of these markets is away from large urban centres and located in a village of a large size. They also tend to operate in a cycle covering a specified number of market places (about 3 or 4) in a week, and having links with one of the central established markets, from where the goods and items are replenished. With this mechanics of operation of weekly markets as a background, we study the pattern of location of weekly markets in the district. There are about 58 weekly markets operating in various parts of the district and the business is conspicuously absent in Pavagada taluk. Turuvekere, Gubbi and Tiptur taluks have a large number of weekly markets. It is obvious from the above discussion that such markets must of necessity operate in patches, filling in the gaps created by the reach of permanent urban market facilities and keeping to a regular schedule in a week. Based on the days on which the markets operate in the 58 odd villages we have attempted to link the market circuits. Except for 6 independent locations which occur in the peripheral parts of the district (therefore presumably parts of circuit operating in adjoining district), others can be linked into a cyclical system (Fig. 4.6). We also notice 3 pairs of weekly markets, one each in Tiptur, Sira and Madhugiri/Koratgere which again perhaps form a part of such markets in the adjoining district.

We are able to identify 13 such circuits where they meet on different days of a week. Their locations are best suited for filling in gaps created by the urban markets (Fig. 4.7). While these are away from urban centres, yet close enough to establish links of the selling itinerants for replenishing their goods.

As indicated earlier from the seller's point of view, despite accumulation of demand over a period of time, they would perfer a large village to locate these periodic markets. In order to check this feature, we have tabulated the population size of the villages where periodic markets operate (Table 4.7).

Conjectural Cycles of Weekly Markets

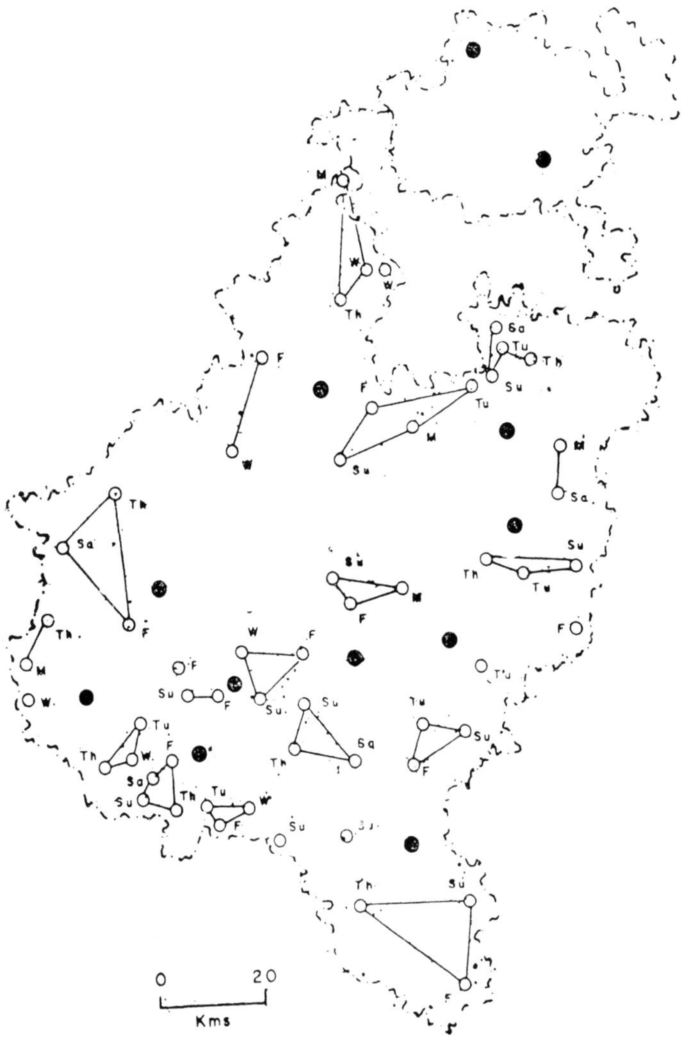

FIG. 4.6

Distribution of Clusters that offer Weekly Market Facilities

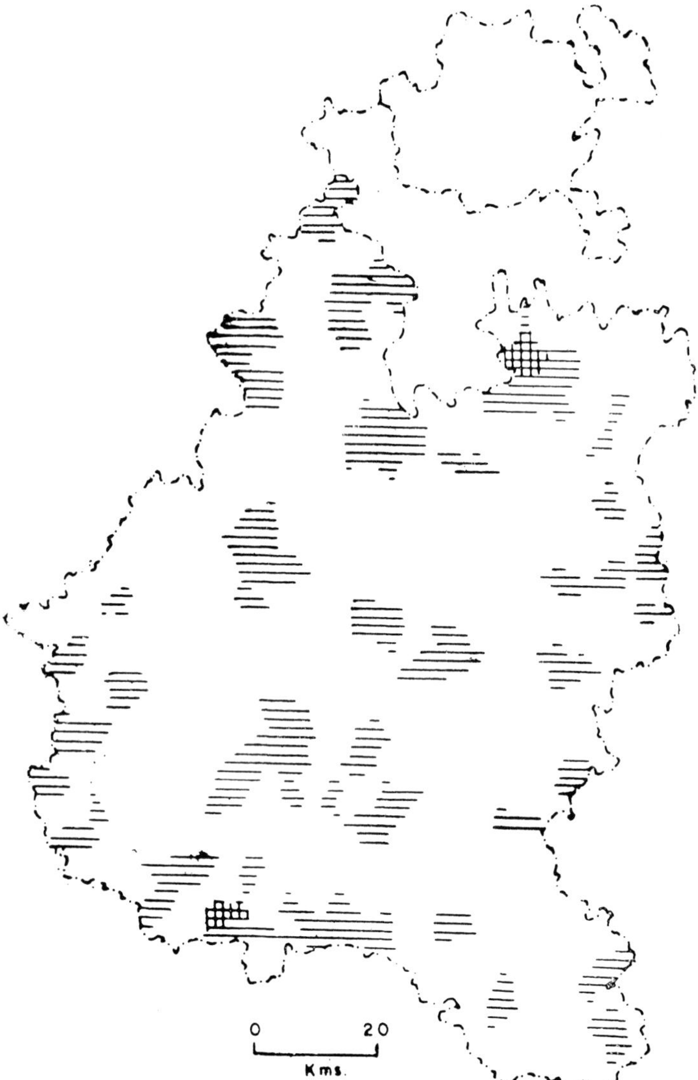

FIG. 4.7

TABLE 4.7

Distribution of villages with weekly markets by population size

Population size class	No. of villages
< 500	3
500-1000	7
1000-2000	23
2000-3000	14
3000-4000	5
4000+	6

Of the 58 markets 48 have more than 1000 population. Roughly 50 per cent of the villages where weekly markets assemble have a population of over 2000.

Pavagada taluk is poorlv placed without any weekly market operating in it (Table 4.8). Turuvekere on the other extreme has 50 per cent of its villages and 60 per cent of its population within a distance of 2 miles from the weekly markets. Tiptur is also similarly placed.

TABLE 4.8

Distance range in availability of weekly markets

Sl. No.	Taluks	Per cent villages (V) and population (P) within					
		2 miles		2-4 miles		Beyond 4 miles	
		V	P	V	P	V	P
1.	C.N. Halli	25	29	32	33	43	38
2.	Gubbi	30	36	48	47	22	17
3.	Koratgere	42	47	42	39	16	14
4.	Kunigal	23	28	49	42	28	30
5.	Madhugiri	30	35	45	34	25	31
6.	Pavagada*	—	—	—	—	—	—
7.	Sira	23	33	51	41	26	26
8.	Tiptur	46	56	52	35	12	9
9.	Tumkur	23	46	48	33	29	21
10.	Turuvekere	50	60	45	32	5	8

* No weekly markets operate in the taluk. (Markets of adjoining district are not included.)

Four of the functions discussed above indicate that a large number of villages are located beyond four miles of their reach. An attempt has been made to identify such areas by combining all the four functions in a single map (Fig. 4.8). Areas which are beyond four miles of all the four functions are seen largely in Pavagada taluk, parts of Sira, C.N. Halli and Kunigal. On the other hand, large parts of Turuvekere and Tiptur are within four miles of all such functions. Southern parts of Sira and northern parts of C.N. Halli show gaps in secondary school facilities. Several parts of the district, however, are beyond four miles of telegraphic services. It is in these areas that future locations of these functions have to be considered.

The Hierarchy of Settlements

Having seen from the above section that many villages depend on a few villages and towns for these six functions we define the importance of the various settlements for the purposes of identifying a settlement hierarchy on the basis of these functions. To these we add the effect of population size as a surrogate for commercial and service activities (other movement attracting functions).

The presence or absence of the functions in the inhabited villages is recorded on a binary scale (using unity or zero). The problem of combining these two dimensions that indicate the importance of a settlement vis-a-vis other settlements has two aspects—the elimination of bias of scale and the weightage of different variables. The aspects may either be dealt with together or separately and at both stages a large number of methods have been used in social science research. Each of thesemethods have one or the other weakness and are only suited for specific problems.

Quite often, the variables chosen in a study vary in their unit of measurement. For example in the present case, whereas the functions listed against settlements take values of 'zero' or 'one', the population varies from less than 30 to over 70,000. Thus, the two facets—functional and population values are not additive until they are made free of bias of scale of measurement. On the other hand, the different functions vary in their importance though the scale of measurement is the same for all (binary). Thus, while they are additive in the statistical

Areas Lying Beyond Four Miles of Central Functions

FIG. 4.8

sense, they are not so while defining settlement hierarchy. Assigning weightage to different functions according to their importance is therefore necessary. Here again, a variety of methods from simple arbitrary assigning of weights to statistical weighting based on relationship between the variables (factor analysis, principal component analysis) are available. We have seen earlier that some functions are found in a large number of settlements while others are less frequent. Thus based on the variance in the distribution of each of the functions weights have been assigned for the six functions, i.e., the greater the variance the greater the weightage of the function. The weighted scores and the population size have then been divided by the respective means of the two series before combining them into a single composite score to indicate the importance or centrality of the settlements.

Based on these composite scores the settlements are grouped into four categories—from the single first order centre (Tumkur) to a large number of fourth order centres at the lower level. The distribution of the centres is mapped in Fig. 4.9. Settlements falling in the first three orders are also listed with their population, functions, and composite scores in Appendix III.

The hierarchy that emerges based on the composite score defines four levels of centres. Of these Tumkur the first order centre stands out markedly from the second order centres with a very high score (142.08) as a result of its size. The scores of the second order centres vary from 31 to 60. Whereas the break in the value between I and II order scores is marked, that between II and III order is less marked and between III and IV it has to be practically defined on the basis of number of centres rather than break in the value of composite score (Appendix III). Other than the first order Tumkur town, 10 other settlements all of which are urban centres are identified as II order. Eighty-four third order centres are also identified including Ammasandra notified area. Obviously some have entered within the first 95 centres (i.e., order I, II and III) because of the population size of functional score or both. The centres in the first two orders are obviously ranked because of both variables, whereas in the third order we fina some because of their size and others because of their functions.

Settlement Hierarchy

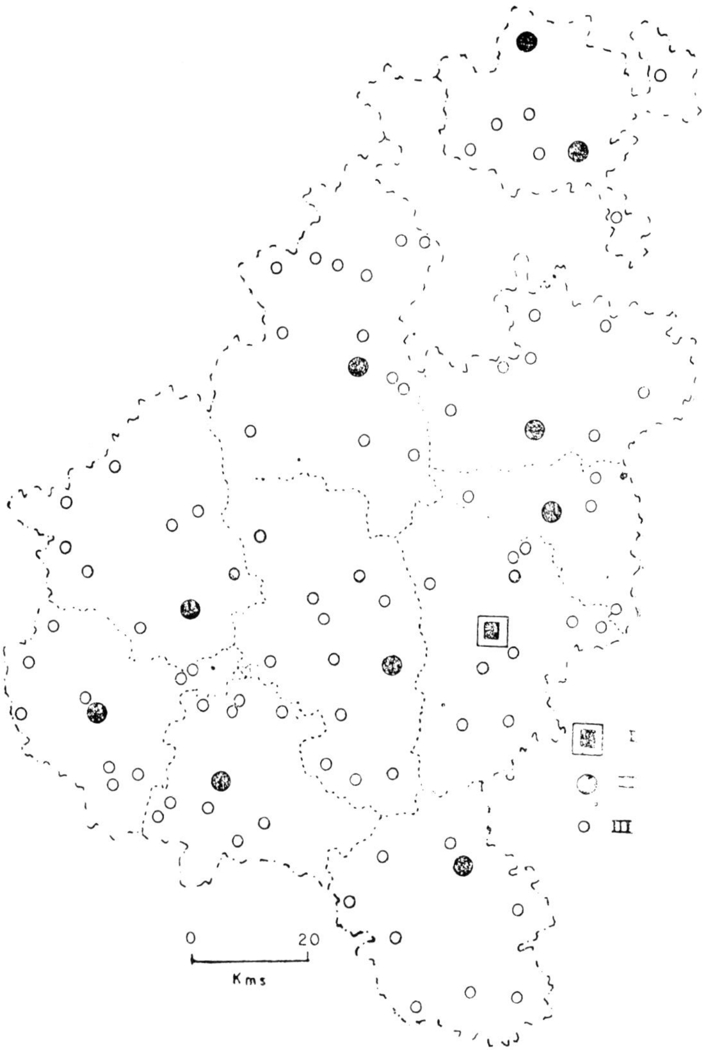

FIG. 4.9

There are a few cases where size and functions do not compare. Generally it is more because of the functional score than population size. Of the ten cases where mutual discrepancy is noted (Appendix III) between population score and functional score, only 4 enter the third order category because of higher score functional despite small population size.

It is also apparent that a few third order centres become redundant since they are located very near a second order settlement (Fig. 4.9). The gaps and overlaps in the availability of functions brought out earlier is supplemented by the distribution pattern of the 95 central places that have been identified. Competitions between the same order centres by virtue of their proximity, particularly, in the case of III order centres also result in overlapping of their hinterlands as indicated in Fig. 4.9.

Level of Intra-Cluster Interactions

Based on the distribution of these functions we estimate the interaction potentials within various clusters. As seen earlier, since the distribution of medical facilities, telegraph offices and weekly markets and secondary schools is restricted to only a few of the 277 clusters in addition to generating movement from within the cluster they must also attract movement from other clusters. For the present, we estimate only movement within the clusters for these functions.

If, however, one finds location of a function in all the villages of a cluster, it would not generate movement for that function from within. On the other extreme if none of the villages has a given function in a cluster then also no movement is likely to take place. In reality most of the cases are in between these extremes. When functions are performed by some of the villages, in a cluster, intra-cluster movements are promoted. To bring out the level of interaction, within various clusters we compute values on the basis of the following assumption. We assume that in the absence of a function in a village the population would move to the nearest place where that function is available (only intra-cluster locations are considered). Under this assumption, levels of intra-cluster

Estimated Levels of Intra-cluster Interactions

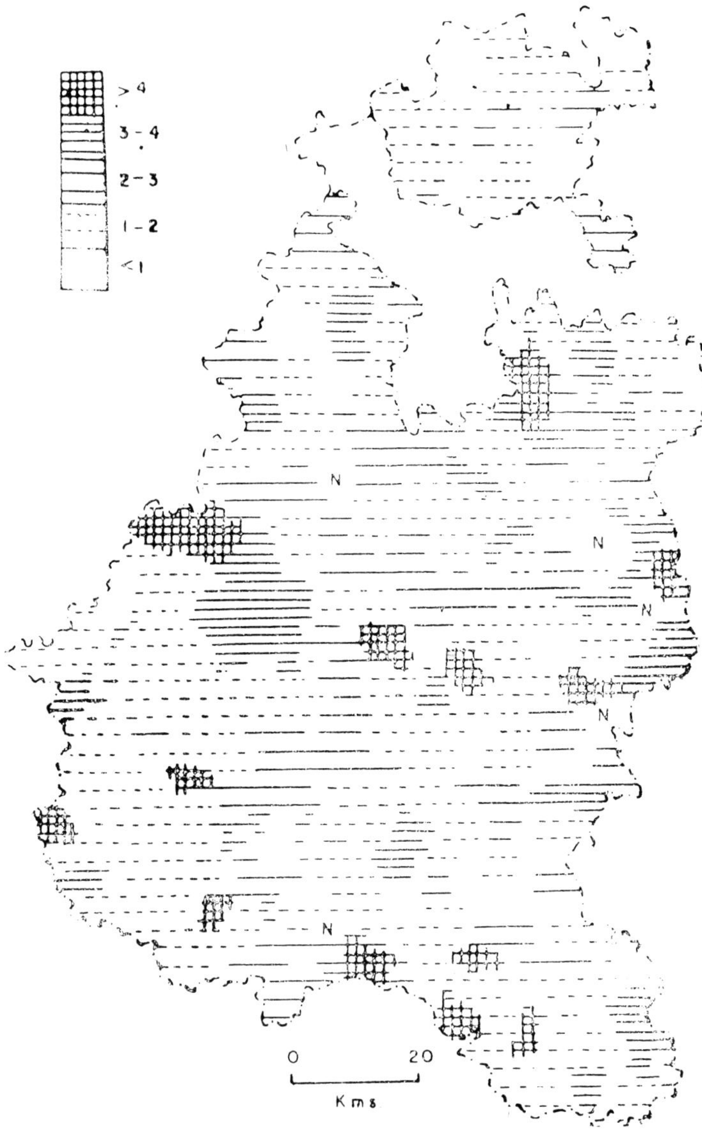

FIG. 4.10

interactions of the i th cluster for the k th function. I_{ck} are computed using the following expression :

$$I_{ck} = \frac{(N_c - N_{ck})}{N_c}$$

where N_c is the number of villages in the cluster, N_{ck} (>o) is the number of villages in the cluster performing the function 'k'. These values have been aggregated for the six functions and mapped in Fig. 4.10.

A study of the map indicates that three clusters do not have any potentials for interaction, all of which are within urban shadow areas. This is one of the extreme situations mentioned earlier—none of the villages in these clusters performing any of the six functions (one—a cluster of 6 villages and the other two with 3 villages each).

About 200 clusters indicate a medium level of interaction (index value of 1-3) whereas 56 clusters indicate a high level of interaction. Most of these 56 clusters are large units with 10 or more villages in each of them of which one or two villages provide all the functions. As seen from table 4.9 the clusters in the urban shadow have lesser potential of interaction when compared to clusters beyond urban shadow areas. Clusters with higher levels of interaction usually occur singly and in different parts of the district. Pavagada, and Sira taluks record less interactions within their clusters.

TABLE 4.9

Distribution of clusters by interaction levels

Index of Interaction	Within urban shadow		Beyond urban shadow	
	Number	Per cent	Number	Per cent
0	3	4.5%	0	0
.01—1	22	25%	3	1.6%
1—2	35	40%	85	44 4%
2—3	19	20%	54	28%
3—4	6	9%	34	18%
4+	2	1.5%	14	8%
Total	87	100%	190	100%

Road Network

Since the facility required for enacting these interactions is the availability of road network, it will be worthwhile to see the distribution of villages with pucca road connections in various clusters. However, since the road network pattern has remained a direct result of the needs of large urban centres, it is to be expected that the network is not geared to rural interaction. Consequently we find that the clusters within urban shadow areas have better pucca road connections as compared to clusters beyond urban shadows (Fig. 4.11). Whereas 60 per cent of the clusters beyond urban shadows have less than 40 per cent of the villages connected by pucca road, only 59 per cent of urban shadow clusters record less than 40 per cent of their villages with road connections. On the other hand whereas 17 per cent of the clusters beyond the urban shadow have above 60 per cent of their villages connected by pucca roads, 26 per cent of the urban shadow clusters have more than 60 per cent of the villages located on pucca roads. (Table 4.10).

TABLE 4.10

Relationship between road availability and levels of interaction

% villages with pucca road	Levels of Interaction						
	0	.01-1	1-2	2-3	3-4	Above 4	Total
0	1	5	22	8	2	0	38
1—20	0	5	22	16	5	3	51
20—40	2	8	36	23	14	7	90
40—60	0	2	14	11	11	4	42
60—80	0	3	20	11	5	1	40
Above 80	0	2	6	4	3	1	16
Total	3	25	120	73	40	16	277

A chi-square test of the availability of pucca road and levels of interaction indicates no relationship between the two.

What is perhaps more revealing is the pattern of road network in the clusters. Does the network connect the villages with each other or not? We have selected four cases where many villages show connections by pucca road and traced out the road network (Fig. 4.12). It is clearly seen from the four cases that the villages are not really connected with each other but they get connected to the road network system since they

Cluster-wise Distribution of per cent villages connected by Pucca Road

FIG. 4.11

lie on the route connecting larger urban centres that are located within or without the cluster. Another pattern of the connection is through a linking of village to the nearest highway (that connects urban centres).

Patterns of Road Network in Selected Clusters

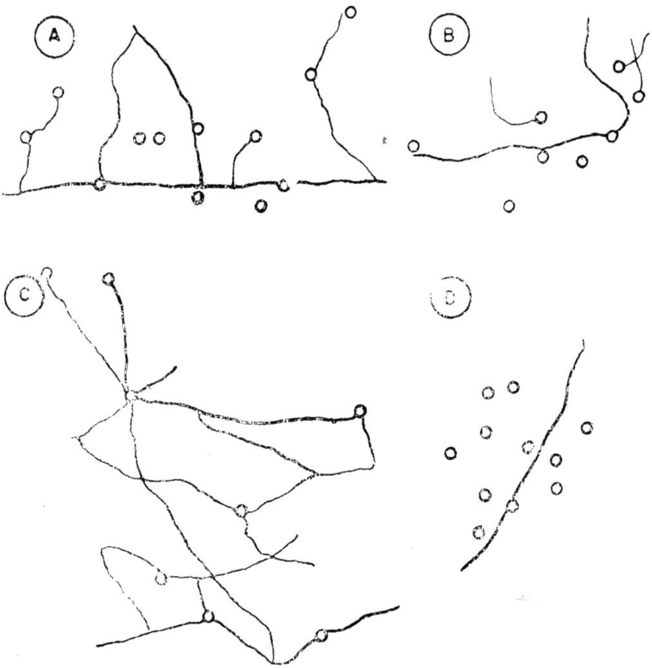

FIG. 4.12

We have argued here that the concept of hierarchical arrangement should not be extended to development strategies but must only be applied to service functions. Spatial gaps and overlaps in some central functions have been brought out. This might be helpful in future locational decisions with reference to these functions. It is also apparent from the above analysis that the existing number of facilities could have been made to bring a larger proportion of villages and population within shorter distances of these functions. The hierarchy of central places identified also brings out such functional and spatial overlaps and gaps. The introduction of the concept of village cluster in this format has resulted in identifying a group of contiguous villages that are not efficiently served by some of these services while contiguous clusters of villages in some parts have better reach to them.

Based on the clusterwise distribution of these functions, intra-cluster movement of people has been estimated. We have indications that a considerable proportion of movement of the rural population is for such public utility services. In fact in the order of frequency of visits, such functions as have been discussed here rank second among a set of six different purposes.[1] In availing the services offered by these functions no distinction in travel pattern is seen between large farmers and small farmers.[2] It is also apparent from the Kanakapura study (more or less a similar tract as Tumkur) that 5-9 kms is the modal distance range of interaction for purchase/sale of articles of household consumption and other amenities discussed above. Also clear from these studies in areas far different inm any attributes, walking, public bus and cycles seen to be the mode of movement for different distance ranges of travel. In the light of these observations, the incompatibility of the existing transport network pattern with the estimated levels of inter-village interaction assumes greater importance. There is then a case for strengthening intervillage interactions through changes in the structure of the rural transport network.

REFERENCES

1. V.L.S. Prakasa Rao, *Development Strategy for an Agricultural Region*, IDS, University of Mysore, Prasanga, 1976, 1.173.
2. S. Madhavan, *Rural Transport in Karnataka with Special Reference to Kanakapura (Bangalore District)*, Polytechnic of Central London, Transport Studies Group, (Mimeo), 1978.

5

Implications For Planning

IF PLANNING for development were only a matter of generating employment, monitoring patterns of investment, providing subsidies and infrastructure of identifying growth poles and centres, we would not, after thirty years of planning, still be explaining the failure of our plans. This is reason enough to question the basic philosophy and strategies of our planning, and to usher in fundamental changes in them. With specific reference to micro-level planning the omission of macro processes that operate in the space economy has left a serious lacuna. The failure of any number of micro-level planning programmes of development in India can be attributed to the treatment of territorial units as a closed system. The dependence on the non-existent diffusion has accentuated regional disparities rather than narrowing them. The application of received theories, like growth poles and core-periphery models though logically sound, to situations which are environmentally incompatible has obviously not produced any results. In the course of their application to the Indian situation, the only alteration is the idea of a hierarchy of diluted poles in the form of growth points and growth centres. Such a concept then has not aided diffusion of impulses from the core to the periphery but has become an instrument of drain of peripheral resources to the cores. In the process the interactions between peripheries and within peripheries have been weakened.

It is not difficult to trace back the connection between the concepts of hierarchy and development strategies of space economy. The concept of hierarchy in the settlement system stated in a formal way can be traced back to Christaller's central place theory wherein the crux of the issue is the distribution of central service functions and spatial organization through such services. Perroux's growth pole concept and Friedman's core-periphery theory dealing with production activities in an economic space and Christaller's model of geographic space inter-mingled and metamorphosed into growth centres and their hierarchy. We fail to see the logic of connection of the two ideas—one which is independent of local resources and the other based on concentration of related activities through geographic inertia, multiplier and agglomeration tendencies based on the resources of its locale.

Evidences have been cited in the preceding chapters supporting the suction mechanism operating in the Indian economy at macro-level through the flow of resources from the resource rich areas to the metropolitan economy. The large-scale public investments have at best aided in hastening this process. Evidences are also available at micro-level wherein a number of village studies indicate the absence of any percolation affect.[1] In the light of these observations we have developed the idea of cluster of villages wherein a group of contiguous villages are looked at as a community with mutual interests. Such a framework, it is hoped will strengthen inter-village interaction and integration and dissipate the growing upward links the villages are forced to establish. A variety of measures including social, economic, political and cultural ones have to be sprouted in order to strengthen inter-village interactions. Obviously, this concept as an instrument of planning for rural development is not oriented to achieve short term targets and planning goals but geared to bring about integrated communities and to usher in fundamental changes in the orientation of our rural economy.

Descending from these theoretical considerations we may now look at what we have accomplished in this empirical study of Tumkur district. We have developed a method of grouping villages into clusters and identified 200 odd clusters of villages in the district. These clusters then have formed the units of our analysis of economy and infrastructure. The analysis of crop patterns has indicated possibilities of grouping these clusters into a second order cluster for purposes of agricultural planning. Areas of commercial agriculture, for example the groundnut/oilseed dominant northern taluks of the district seem to be worse off in many ways. Do we then conclude that commercialisation of agriculture leads to backwardness ? The negative impacts of commercialisation have also been observed elsewhere, wherein it has been found that the shift to groundnut cropping introduced the activities of trading families who lent finances and acquired the crop yields in return. The rental as well as trading surpluses were drained off.[2] This also gives a warning to the proposed schemes of sericulture development in the southern parts of the district. These aspects have to be taken into account if desired results are to be achieved. The role of household industries is seen to be diminishing. While there is a need for strengthening this sector, much care is needed to make sure that the income generated by this sector does not fall within the money-lender-trader combine. This needs an effective institutional organization. Such organization can be thought of at the level of village clusters which provides thresholds in terms of the strength of the work force, and available pooled infrastructure.

The weak manufacturing base of the district may be strengthened, both in urban as well as rural sectors. The existing manufacturing activities of the rural sector are found to be agriculture/livestock based. The urban manufacturing activities may be oriented towards providing input requirements of the rural sector.

The predominance of agriculture in the rural economy and of tertiary activities in the urban economy is apparent. The redistributive role played by the urban centres is convincingly brought out by the fact that the first three dominant commodities exported by them happen to be agricultural products (Table 5.1). The imports into these towns again are construction materials and agricultural implements (the former an urban product and the latter meant for consumption in the rural sector) in addition to agricultural products. It is also apparent from the items manufactured in these urban places, that the produce is geared to serve urban consumption. In effect, the urban centres are producing for urban market and control the exchange of rural products. Such a situation then creates doubts as to whether urbanization can be considered a developmental indicator. While the Collin Clark[3] hypothesis gives

TABLE 5.1

Major commodities produced, shipped and received by urban centres in Tumkur district

Sl. No.	Name of Town	Manufactured	Shipped	Received
1.	Ammasandra (NAC)	Cement	Cement	Coal, Gunny Bags, Gypsum
2.	Chiknayakanahalli	Coarse Woollen blankets, silk sarees	Copra, Arecanut, Coconut	Wool, Silk Yarn, Cloth
3.	Gubbi	Bullock Carts, Handloom sarees and Dhotis	Mango fruits, Coconuts, Arecanuts	Salt, Edible Oil, Cloth
4.	Koratgere	Pottery	Rice, Groundnut, Jaggery	Cloth, Agricultural Implements, Fertilizers
5.	Kunigal	Beedies, Agricultural Implements, Silk Yarn	Jaggery, Paddy, Silkworm cocoons	Jaggery, Paddy, silkworm cocoons
6.	Madhugiri	Castor Oil	Groundnuts, Paddy, Arecanut	Ragi, Rice, Horsegram.
7.	Pavagada	Groundnut Oil, soap, steel furniture	Groundnut seeds and oil, Foodgrains, Tobacco Leaves	Steel, Diesel, Petrol, Kerosene, Timber
8.	Sira	Coarse woollen blankets, Beedies	Tobacco, Paddy, Onion	Cloth, Sugar, Ragi
9.	Tiptur	Coir rugs, Matchsticks, coir	Copra, Broomsticks, Coconut oil	Rice, Ragi, Jaggery.
10.	Tumkur	Agricultural Implements, soapnut powder, Wooden furniture	Tamarind, Soapnut powder, Arecanut	Cloth, Jaggery, Arecanut
11.	Turuvekere	—	Copra, Coconuts, Broomsticks	Cloth, Agricultural Implements
12.	Y.N. Hoskote	Coarse Woollen blankets, Art silk cloth, Handloom cloth	Groundnuts, Tamarind, Coarse woollen blankets	Cement, Kerosene, Art Silk

Source : District Census Handbook, Tumkur District, Census of India, 1971.

credence to the consideration of urbanisation as an index of development, particularly in terms of the services/sector, we must realise that western countries which are characterised by high proportions of tertiary workers, have passed through a stage of development of the secondary sector while developing countries have bypassed that stage. Under the circumstances where the sequence of occupational shifts entails a bypassing of dominance in the secondary sector, a consideration of urban population as an indicator of development has to be reconsidered. Even the argument that urbanization leads to modernization as opposed to tradition, does not hold good since our modern sector is not as modern, nor our traditional sector as traditional.

Provision of amenities is an instrument in strengthening rural community idea within the format of village clusters. The concentration of such amenities in a few centres aids the dependence of villages on such higher order places for the services they require. Such concentration doubtless increases the efficiency of the delivery system. However, we may also think of dispersing certain lower order functions (that are expected to cater to 10 to 15 villages) among the villages in order to strengthen inter-village interactions. Such scattering of functions including provision of platforms for social gatherings, entertainment, rural sports etc., may aid strengthening interaction among villages. From our analysis it is apparent that the average distance range of some of these functions is about 7 kilometres. Dispersal of these services necessarily increases aggregate travel distances. This may not be a serious constraint, since the total distances are small, and the mode of transport (by foot, cycles, bullock carts) consumes no fuel energy. Walking and cycling being the normal mode of movement of people for such distance ranges (and likely to remain so for decades to come) the increased travel distances do not entail enhanced monetary costs. Also many of these functions are independent services in the sense that they cannot be availed of in multipurpose visits (say medical facilities and telegraph/post offices).

The working of the village clusters also necessitates structural changes in the pattern of road network. We have brought out on the basis of the existing pattern of road network development, that availability of pucca roads to villages merely means the location of a village on a highway connecting some urban places, or the villages in some cases are linked to the highway to be drawn into the urban influence zone. Inter-village roads may be thought of as a means to promote interactions among neighbouring villages.

The study presented here is obviously not a comprehensive treatise on micro-level planning for rural development. Some of the basic problems with our micro-level planning have been indicated. While raising a number of issues pertaining to this an alternative has been put forward. It is also realised that several aspects are not even mentioned. With the help of the large set of household data covering a variety of aspects of rural society and economy on Tumkur district villages, such aspects are expected to be analysed in the series of studies that are in progress and planned.

Appendices

Appendix 1

Location Code of the Constituent Villages

Cluster No.	Taluk	Inhabited	Un-inhabited
1	2	3	4
1	Pavagada	120, 121, 122, 124	—
2	,,	123, 125, 126, 127	—
3	,,	115, 116, 117, 128, 129, 130, 131.	118
4	,,	135, 137 to 144	—
6	,,	41, 84, 85, 87, 88, 89, 136	—
8	,,	8 to 15	
9	,,	23 to 25, 44, 46 to 49	
10	,,	42, 43, 45, 50, 51	
11	,,	35, 38, 57, 58	39, 40, 59
12	,,	34, 68 to 72, 98, 99, 100	36, 37
13	,,	101 to 106	—
14	,,	62 to 67	—
15	,,	52 to 56	60, 61
16	Sira	243 to 246, 249	—
17	,,	235 to 242	—
18	,,	207 to 211, 247, 248	—
19	,,	218 to 223, 231 to 234	—
20	,,	212 to 217	—
21	,,	224 to 230	—

1	2	3	4
22	Sira	204 to 206	—
23	,,	201 to 203	—
24	,,	47, 170, 171	—
25	,,	169, 185, 186, 198 to 200	—
26	,,	188 to 197	184, 187
27	,,	176 to 178, 180, 181	179, 182
28	,,	39 to 41, 172 to 175, 183	—
30	Sira Madhugiri	16 to 20, 22, 23 316	—
31	Madhugiri	243 to 250, 252, 253	251
32	,,	254, 255, 262 to 264	—
33	,,	28 to 33, 256 to 261	—
34	,,	23, 25, 26, 27, 34, 35, 36, 183	22
35	,,	68, 76, 78, 79, 80, 81, 90	200, 77, 189 192, 194
36	,,	17 to 21, 37, 39 to 43, 1, 4	3, 15, 16, 38
37	,,	44 to 46, 48 to 52	47
38	,,	2, 5 to 12, 14	—
39	,,	53, 82 to 86	13
40	,,	55, 61 to 65, 93, 94	54, 95
41	,,	56 to 60, 96, 99	—
42	,,	100 to 104, 107	105, 106
43	,,	90, 91, 92, 97, 98	—
44	,,	108 to 112, 114, 115	113, 116
45	,,	66, 67, 69 to 75	—
46	,,	87, 88, 89, 124, 125, 128	
47	,,	117 to 122, 143, 147	—
48	,,	123, 126, 137, to 140	

1	2	3	4
		142, 144 to 146, 148, 164	130, 141
49	Madhugiri	131 to 136, 193	127
50	,,	129, 165 to 172, 174, 175, 196, 197, 199, 205	173, 195, 198, 219
52	,,	239 to 241, 265, 266, 268, 269, 270 to 276	267
53	,,	300 to 310, 314, 315, 317, 318, 319, 320	277, 278, 301, 311, 312
54	,,	279, 280, 281, 283, 285, 289, 290, 291, 293 to 299, 313	282, 284, 286, 287, 288, 292
55	Sira	21, 55, 57 to 63, 65 to 69, 71 to 73	56
56	,,	52, 97, 98, 99	—
57	,,	106, 109, 110, 111, 114 to 118	107, 112
58	,,	31, 32, 108, 159, 160, 161, 165, 166	—
59	,,	36, 37, 38, 155 to 158	—
60	,,	148, 153, 162 to 164, 167, 168	147, 151, 152, 154
61	C.N. Hall i	155 to 158	—
62	,,	140 to 145, 154	—
63	,,	151, 152, 153, 159 to 161, 163, 200	162, 201
64	Sira	100, 101, 136 to 139, 142	249, 135, 140, 141
	Gubbi	251, 252	
65	Sira	102 to 105, 132 to 134	
66	,,	113, 119 to 125, 127, 128, 129, 130	126, 131
	Gubbi	275, 276	

1	2	3	4
67	Sira	64, 70, 75, 84, 86 to 89, 91 to 96	—
68	,,	74, 76 to 83	—
	Koratgere	235 to 240	—
69	Koratgere	228 to 230, 233, 234, 242, 244 to 250	241, 243
70	,,	221 to 227, 231, 232	—
72	,,	13 to 17, 19, 195	—
73	,,	50 to 56, 60, 65, 66, 18	21, 22, 49
74	Madhugiri	149 to 157, 159 to 163	158
75	Koratgere	57 to 59, 61, 62, 64	—
76	,,	63, 67 to 74, 77, 109	76
77	,,	48, 97 to 100, 104, 108, 110	—
78	,,	75, 78 to 94, 111 to 115, 117	193
79	,,	118 to 122, 125, 126, 116, 151, 153, 190 to 192	124, 152
80	,,	123, 127, 128, 130 144 to 147, 149, 150, 155	129, 143
81	Koratgere	131, 134 to 139, 141, 142	132, 133, 140
	Tumkur	70, 72, 73, 74, 67, 68, 69	
82	,,	63, 65, 66, 71, 76, 77, 79 to 82, 84, 85, 86	78, 83
83	,,	64, 119	—
	Koratgere	148, 154, 156, 157, 159, 160, 162 to 166	—

1	2	3	4
84	Koratgere	167 to 171, 177 to 179, 184 to 189	—
85	Tumkur	166, 168, 141, 171 to 175, 180	164, 165, 167, 170
86	,,	149 to 152, 148, 144, 146, 142, 138, 292, 162, 163, 169	139, 145, 147, 153, 160, 161
87	,,	154, 155, 157, 158, 159, 299, 300, 301, 302	156
	Sira	85, 90	
88	Gubbi	250, 271, 272, 281, 273, 282, 283, 285, 277, 335, 338, 339, 341 to 346	278, 279, 284, 336, 340
89	Gubbi	232, 233, 234, 236, 238, 239, 245, 246, 248	235, 237, 241, 243, 247
90	C.N. Halli	202 to 205, 209, 226, 168, 198, 199, 227, 229, 230, 35	206, 207, 208
91	,,	193, 194, 196, 197, 228, 232, 233	234
92	,,	137, 138, 139, 146 to 190, 164 to 167, 169, 170, 171, 173	—
93	,,	183, 190, 191, 192	—
94	,,	82, 135, 184 to 189	—
95	,,	126 to 134	
96	,,	80, 81, 123, 124, 125	—
97	,,	84 to 90, 180	—
98	,,	136, 181, 182	—
99	,,	91 to 94, 172, 174 to 179, 231	—
100	,,	23, 95 to 100, 103, 111	22, 101

1	2	3	4
101	C.N. Halli	104, 105, 106, 107, 109, 110, 112, 113	—
102	,,	114 to 122	—
103	Tiptur	86 to 95, 97, 98, 99	96
104	,,	77 to 85, 102	—
105	,,	100, 101, 103, 104, 105, 106, 115, 116	—
106	,,	107, 109, 110, 111, 113, 114	108, 112
107	C.N. Halli	19, 21, 26, 41, 43, 72 to 7[illegible], 108	20
109	C.N. Halli	212 to 219	—
	Gubbi	195, 196, 227, 257,	197, 226, 228
110	Gubbi	254, 258, 259, 266, 267, 269, 296, 297, 270, 332	255, 242, 244, 256, 261, 268, 274
111	,,	286 to 288, 290 to 295, 298, 333, 334	—
112	,,	320, 321, 323 to 330	—
113	Tumkur	296, 297, 298, 304 to 307, 309, 310, 278	303, 308
115	,,	341 to 345, 347 to 357, 359	—
116	,,	250, 254, 255, 360, 361, 363 to 367, 358	—
117	,,	368 to 372, 375, 214, 218, 219, 233, 234, 237, 238, 251	—
118	,,	217, 220, 221, 240, 241, 242, 262, 263, 271, 272, 273	—
	Gubbi	35, 36, 39, 40, 41	
120	Gubbi	17, 18, 308, 310,	

1	2	3	4
		311, 314, 316, 317, 318	309
121	Gubbi	176, 163, 263, 264, 289, 300, 301 to 305, 322	260, 306
122	,,	13, 14, 166 to 169, 171, 173, 174, 175	170, 185
123	,,	184, 186, 189, 190, 192, 193, 191, 200	187, 188
124	,,	198, 199, 201 to 210	172
125	,,	214, 217, 218, 220 to 225, 229, 230, 231	—
126	Tiptur	140, 141, 145, 148, 150, 151, 152, 147	142, 146
127	Tiptur	136, 138, 139	137
	C.N. Halli	49, 60 to 68	
128	C.N. Halli	10, 11, 44 to 48, 49, 70, 71	69
129	Tiptur	8, 127, 128, 131, 133, 134, 135, 157, 158, 159	126
131	,,	70 to 74, 69	—
132	,,	54, 55, 61 to 65, 67, 68, 75, 76	—
133	,,	45 to 53	—
134	,,	32 to 40, 44	—
135	,,	27, 28, 29. 31, 195, 225 to 228	—
136	,,	176 to 179, 188, 192 to 194, 196, 197, 198	—
137	,,	160, 161, 164 to 168, 170, 175	—
138	,,	133, 134, 135, 157 to 159	—

1	2	3	4
139	Tiptur	155, 156, 143, 144, 153	154
	Turuvekere	23, 24, 25, 30	
141	Gubbi	99, 100, 103, 211, 212, 213	101, 102
142	,,	96, 98, 104, 106, 107, 152 to 157, 159, 160, 161	105, 128
143	,,	109 to 112, 115, 116, 162	—
145	,,	42 to 44, 67, 122, 124, 126	—
146	Gubbi	74	72, 73, 75
	Tumkur	202, 206 to 211, 259, 239, 256	207, 258
147	Tumkur	212, 213, 215, 252, 243, 244, 246, 257, 261	216
148	,,	230 to 232, 245, 247 to 249	—
149	,,	197, 198, 199, 200, 201, 203, 204, 222, 226 to 229	—
150	Tumkur	223 to 225	
	Gubbi	76, 80, 81	
	Kunigal	70	
151	Gubbi	63, 64, 69 to 71, 79, 84 to 88	77, 78
152	,,	56, 66, 68, 125, 127 to 130	—
153	,,	132, 134, 136 to 141, 148 to 151	135, 142
154	,,	89 to 92, 120, 121, 143 to 147	
155	Gubbi	93, 94, 95, 108	
	Turuvekere	89 to 90	
156	Turuvekere	79, 83, 84, 85, 86	91
	Gubbi	97	

1	2	3	4
157	Turuvekere	47, 49, 50, 92, 100, 101, 103 to 106	48, 102
159	Tiptur	172	
	Turuvekere	12, 14 to 22, 35, 37, 41	—
160	Tiptur	171, 173, 180 to 187, 199	—
161	,,	215, 217 to 224. 229	—
162	,,	209, 211 to 214, 216	210
163	,,	201 to 208	—
164	Tiptur	200	
	Turuvekere	4, 5, 11, 208 to 211	10
165	Turuvekere	203 to 207, 212, 213, 220	214
166	,,	197 to 199, 201, 202, 215 to 219, 224 to 226, 241	—
167	,,	190 to 194, 196, 238, 242, 243	195, 237
168	,,	232 to 236, 239, 127, 179, 180	178
169	,,	126, 130, 134, 135, 175 to 177, 181 to 184, 187 to 189	—
170	,,	166 to 174	—
171	,,	136 to 140, 142, 143, 149, 150, 164, 185, 186	—
172	,,	93 to 97, 99, 141	98
173	Turuvekere	144 to 148	—
	Gubbi	59, 131, 133	54
174	Gubbi	53, 55, 57, 58, 60, 61, 62	65
175	Turuvekere	153 to 156, 162, 163, 165	151, 152
176	Kunigal	55 to 59, 297, 307, 309 to 312	65
177	Kunigal	67 to 69, 71, 63, 64, 313	—

1	2	3	4
	Gubbi	82, 83	
	Tumkur	205	
178	Kunigal	72 to 85	—
180	,,	42, 54, 264 to 269, 296	262, 263
181	,,	292 to 295, 298, 299, 301 to 306, 291	300, 308
182	Kunigal	282, 284 to 290	
	Turuvekere	147 to 160	161
183	Kunigal	233 to 238, 251 to 256, 275, 277	250, 273
184	Kunigal	257, 270 to 272, 278, 280, 181	279
185	,,	227 to 230, 232, 239, 243 to 246	231
186	,,	247 to 249, 258, 259	—
187	,,	13 to 16, 19 to 25	—
188	,,	9 to 12, 96 to 98, 131 to 133, 187	—
189	,,	94, 95, 102, 114 to 121	113
190	,,	93, 112, 123 to 139, 189	—
191	,,	140, 142 to 144, 181 to 184	—
192	,,	17, 18, 176 to 180, 188	185, 186
193	,,	195 to 199, 209 and 210	—
194	Kunigal	190 to 194, 218, 219, 240 to 242	—
195	,,	220 to 226	—
196	,,	208, 211 to 213, 215 to 218	214
197	,,	173, 200 to 207	—
198	,,	134, 167 to 169, 171, 172, 174, 175	170
199	,,	161 to 166	—
200	,,	135 to 139, 141, 145, 146, 148, 160	—
201	,,	147, 149, 151 to 153	—
202	,,	154 to 159	

1	2	3	4
		Clusters in the Urban Influence Zones	
5a	Pavagada	73, 110 to 114	—
5b	,,	74 to 78, 80, 81	—
5c	,,	107 to 109	—
5d	,,	82, 83, 90, 91	—
5e	Pavagada	92 to 97	—
7a	,,	30 to 33, 132, 134	—
7b	,,	1, 3, 133	2
7c	,,	26 to 29	—
7d	,,	16, 18 to 22	—
7e	,,	4 to 7, 17	—
29a	Sira	5, 6, 48 to 51	—
29b	,,	2, 43, 45, 46	3
29c	,,	33, 34, 35, 42, 44	—
29d	,,	27, 28, 30	—
29e	,,	4, 8 to 10, 12 to 15, 17, 24, 25, 29	1, 11
51a	Madhugiri	177, 179, 182, 184 to 188, 201 to 204, 208 to 210	—
51b	,,	181, 227 to 229, 231 to 235	230, 236, 237
51c	,,	176, 207, 211 to 213, 221, 222, 226, 238	—
51d	,,	220, 223 to 225	—
51e	,,	214, 216 to 218	215, 219
71a	Koratgere	189, 196, 197, 200 to 203, 205, 206, 251	199
71b	,,	5, 6, 9, 10, 12, 23	7, 11
71c	,,	8, 20, 24, 25, 27 to 31	3
71d	,,	33, 37, 48, 102, 103, 105 to 107	39
71e	,,	1, 2, 4, 32, 34, 38, 46, 47	35
71f	,,	204, 207, 208, 210, 211, 213, 214 to 218, 220	209, 210, 219

1	2	3	4
71g	,,	42, 44, 45, 172 to 176, 212	48
108a	C.N. Halli	210, 211, 220, 222, 224, 225	221, 223
108b	,,	30, 33, 34, 37, 38	36, 39
108c	,,	15, 16, 17, 18, 24 to 26, 28, 29	27, 31
108d	,,	9, 12, 13, 42	—
108e	C.N. Halli	5 to 8, 14, 50, 51, 52	—
108f	,,	53 to 59	—
114a	Tumkur	276, 284, 289, 298, 311	294, 295
114b	,,	45, 48, 122, 123, 125 to 133, 134, 288, 291	46, 135, 137, 140
114c	,,	186 to 196	134
114d	,,	116, 118, 120, 121	105, 117
114e	,,	37 to 40, 42 to 44, 49, 51, 58	—
114f	,,	3, 4, 5, 42, 50, 56, 57, 59, 60, 61, 62, 317, 318	55
114g	,,	53, 54, 312	124, 293
114h	,,	275, 279 to 283, 287, 313, 322, 326	277, 285
114i	,,	315, 316, 319, 320, 323 to 325, 327	—
114j	,,	11, 12, 13, 14, 15, 321, 392	16
114k	,,	1, 2, 6, 7, 9, 10, 22, 23, 24, 25, 329	8
114 l	,,	26 to 30, 34 to 36, 41, 102 to 104, 106, 107, 111 to 114	31, 32, 33, 110
114m	,,	87, 88, 91 to 93	—
114n	,,	89, 90, 94 to 97, 100, 101, 108, 109, 340	—
114o	,,	98, 99, 328, 330,	

1	2	3	4
		332 to 337, 339, 378 to 381, 393, 395	—
114p	,,	346, 373, 374, 376, 377	—
114q	,,	382, 383, 384, 387, 388	—
114r	,,	17, 268, 269, 270, 274, 385, 389, 390, 391, 394	—
114s	,,	18, 19, 20, 264, 265, 266, 267	—
114t	,,	176 to 179, 181 to 185	—
119a	Gubbi	11, 12, 312, 313, 315	—
119b	,,	16, 19, 20, 21, 22, 24, 25, 28	23
119c	,,	26, 30, 31, 32, 33	27
119d	,,	4 to 7, 10, 29	—
119e	,,	8, 9, 163, 164, 165	—
119f	,,	2, 3, 51, 52, 113, 114	1
119g	,,	34, 38, 48, 50	—
130a	Tiptur	4, 5, 6, 7, 118, 119	—
130b	,,	117, 120, 123, 124, 125	—
130c	,,	60, 66, 121, 122	—
130d	,,	41, 56, 57	42
130e	,,	1, 2, 3, 15, 16, 21, 58, 59	—
130f	,,	9, 12, 14, 17, 18, 20, 174, 230	—
130g	,,	10, 11, 13, 19, 129, 130, 132, 162, 163, 169	—
130h	,,	22 to 26, 30, 43, 189, 190, 181	—
140a	Turuvekere	72, 74, 75, 78	—
	Tiptur	49	—
	Gubbi	216, 219	—
140b	Turuvekere	27, 28, 29, 71	—
140c	,,	26, 31, 32, 33, 34, 49, 121	120
140d	,,	65, 66, 70, 114, 117, 123, 124	68, 69, 125
140e	,,	77, 78, 80, 82, 116	76, 81

1	2	3	4
140f	,,	107, 108, 109, 110, 111, 113, 115, 118	112
158a	,,	2, 3, 6 to 9, 13	—
158b	,,	39, 40, 42 to 45	—
158c	,,	46, 51, 56	52
158d	,,	1, 55, 60, 62, 63, 64	54, 53
158e	,,	57, 58, 59	129, 131, 133
158f	,,	61, 128, 229, 230, 231, 240	—
158g	,,	221, 222, 223, 227	—
179a	Kunigal	9, 66, 86 to 89	90
179b	,,	41, 44, 45, 46, 51, 52, 53, 60, 62	—
179c	,,	1, 2, 47, 92, 108	49, 50, 107
179d	,,	101, 103 to 106, 109 to 111	—
179e	,,	3, 4, 5, 7, 8, 33 to 38, 99, 100	6
179f	,,	24, 26, 27, 28, 30, 31, 32	29, 39

Appendix II

Selected characteristics of Clusters

Cluster No.	No. of villages		Total population	Total workers	Crop combinations
	Inhabited	Un-inhabited			
1	2	3	4	5	6
1	4	—	5977	2445	Oilseeds, Millets, Jowar.
2	4	—	4339	1757	Millets, Jowar, Oilseeds.
3	8	1	5114	2026	Jowar, Oilseeds, Millets.
4	9	—	4484	2707	Oilseeds, Jowar.
6	7	—	5980	2801	Oilseeds, Jowar.
8	8	—	10,012	4380	Oilseeds, Ragi, Jowar.
9	8	—	8477	3592	Oilseeds, Millets.
10	5	—	6513	2892	Oilseeds, Millets, Ragi.
11	4	3	5227	1139	Oilseeds
12	9	2	7495	3073	Oilseeds
13	6	—	6282	2688	Millets, Oilseeds, Jowar.
14	6	—	6136	2555	Multicrop
15	5	2	4297	1766	Millets, Oilseeds, Ragi.
16	5	—	5421	1956	Millets.
17	8	—	5918	2126	Millets, Ragi, Jowar.
18	7	—	5674	1724	Millets, Ragi.
19	10	—	6589	2220	Multicrop

(Contd.)

1	2	3	4	5	6
20	6	—	3678	1295	Multicrop
21	7	—	2986	1340	Millets, Oilseeds.
22	3	—	6110	2116	Millets, Ragi.
23	3	—	8007	2898	Millets, Jowar, Ragi
24	3	—	3989	1389	Millets, Ragi.
25	6	—	3178	1167	Jowar, Millets.
26	10	2	6435	2140	Multicrop
27	5	2	3981	1315	Multicrop
28	8	—	5297	1657	Millets, Ragi, Rice.
30	8	—	6627	2614	Ragi, Oilseeds.
31	10	1	6685	3087	Ragi, Oilseeds.
32	5	—	4484	2048	Oilseeds, Ragi
33	12	—	4274	1673	Oilseeds, Ragi.
34	8	1	5014	1924	Oilseeds, Ragi, Millets.
35	7	6	5050	2255	Oilseeds, Millets, Ragi.
36	13	4	7398	2480	Oilseeds, Ragi, Rice.
37	8	1	5338	2142	Oilseeds, Ragi, Millets
38	10	—	6157	2885	Oilseeds, Ragi, Rice.
39	6	1	5683	2238	Multicrop
40	7	2	4409	1798	Ragi, Millets, Jowar.
41	7	—	4592	1780	Multicrop

1	2	3	4	5	6
42	6	2	6309	2681	Multicrop
43	5	—	4267	1546	Multicrop
44	7	2	8059	3157	Multicrop
45	9	—	3713	2000	Oilseeds, Ragi, Millets.
46	6	—	7706	2815	Ragi, Millets.
47	8	2	7228	2735	Ragi, Oilseeds.
48	12	2	9186	3759	Ragi, Oilseeds, Rice.
49	7	1	4843	2007	Oilseeds, Ragi
50	15	4	6941	2656	Oilseeds, Ragi.
52	14	1	8980	3465	Ragi, Oilseeds.
53	16	5	6910	2628	Ragi
54	16	6	5651	1933	Ragi, Oilseeds.
55	19	1	5295	1892	Ragi, Millets, Oilseeds
56	4	—	9982	3312	Multicrop
57	9	2	4061	1425	Millets, Oilseeds, Ragi.
58	8	—	3231	1063	Millets
59	7	—	1604	502	Multicrop
60	7	4	3643	1235	Oilseeds, Millets.
61	4	—	4581	1739	Ragi, Oilseeds.
62	7	—	4422	1506	Ragi, Millets.
63	8	2	5586	1943	Ragi

(*Contd.*)

1	2	3	4	5	6
64	9	4	7796	2350	Multicrop
65	7	—	4258	1353	Multicrop
66	14	2	3940	1294	Oilseeds, Ragi, Millets.
67	14	—	6957	3543	Ragi, Oilseeds, Millets.
68	15	—	3737	1301	Ragi, Millets, Oilseeds.
69	13	2	5116	1918	Ragi
70	9	—	5020	1838	Ragi
72	7	—	3131	1006	Oilseeds, Ragi.
73	11	3	7541	3121	Oilseeds, Ragi, Rice.
74	14	1	8003	2927	Oilseeds, Ragi, Rice.
75	6	—	6124	1285	Millets, Oilseeds.
76	11	1	4367	1600	Ragi, Millets.
77	8	—	6811	2897	Ragi, Oilseeds, Rice.
78	24	1	5806	2256	Ragi, Oilseeds.
79	13	2	3932	1137	Ragi, Oilseeds.
80	11	2	4537	1447	Ragi, Oilseeds.
81	16	3	4887	1573	Ragi
82	13	2	9151	2982	Ragi.
83	16	—	4029	1698	Oilseeds, Ragi.
84	14	—	5378	1827	Oilseeds, Ragi.
85	9	4	4274	1524	Ragi

1	2	3	4	5	6
86	13	6	5872	2309	Ragi
87	11	1	4015	1373	Ragi, Millets, Oilseeds.
88	10	5	5369	1845	Ragi, Oilseeds.
89	10	5	5782	1961	Ragi
90	13	3	8428	3121	Ragi
91	7	1	5013	1572	Ragi
92	16	—	6089	2084	Ragi
93	4	—	6648	2175	Ragi
94	8	—	6165	1954	Ragi
95	9	—	5556	1761	Ragi
96	5	—	4374	1204	Ragi
97	8	—	5140	1535	Ragi
98	3	—	8280	2483	Ragi
99	12	—	6242	2181	Ragi
100	10	2	6482	2393	Ragi
101	8	—	4240	1247	Ragi
102	9	—	5901	1808	Ragi, Jowar.
103	13	1	5113	1637	Ragi
104	10	—	3490	1110	Ragi
105	8	—	5710	1945	Ragi
106	6	2	2632	828	Ragi

(Contd.)

1	2	3	4	5	6
107	14	1	6849	2222	Ragi
109	12	3	4838	1748	Ragi
110	10	7	6874	2170	Ragi
111	12	—	7683	2550	Ragi
112	10	—	3204	1132	Ragi
113	10	2	2841	1207	Ragi
115	17	—	5423	1942	Ragi
116	11	—	7039	2450	Ragi
117	14	—	9276	3045	Ragi, Rice.
118	16	—	7896	2917	Ragi
120	12	1	5915	2212	Ragi, Rice.
121	18	2	6888	2240	Ragi
122	18	2	6407	1926	Ragi
123	7	2	3482	1099	Ragi
124	12	1	4460	1397	Ragi
125	12	—	5854	2106	Ragi
126	8	2	5855	1916	Ragi
127	13	1	4069	1392	Ragi
128	10	1	7801	2491	Ragi
129	10	1	4400	1325	Ragi
131	6	—	5957	1604	Ragi
132	11	—	3766	1496	Ragi

1	2	3	4	5	6
133	9	—	5784	2106	Ragi
134	10	—	5697	1635	Ragi
135	9	—	6601	2187	Ragi
136	11	—	4434	1495	Ragi
137	9	—	3359	1118	Ragi
138	6	—	6474	919	Ragi
139	9	1	6474	2334	Ragi, Rice.
141	6	2	2246	663	Ragi, Millets.
142	14	2	7107	2109	Ragi, Millets.
143	7	—	2963	1140	Ragi, Rice
144	7	1	2953	1023	Ragi
145	8	—	6284	2126	Ragi
146	11	4	7450	2297	Ragi, Rice
147	10	1	4462	1924	Ragi
148	7	—	2540	903	Ragi
149	12	—	6641	2166	Ragi, Rice
150	7	—	3539	1206	Ragi, Rice
151	11	2	8412	2872	Ragi, Rice
152	8	—	3560	1306	Ragi
153	12	2	9706	3108	Ragi, Rice

(Contd.)

1	2	3	4	5	6
154	11	—	6285	2182	Ragi
155	8	—	4394	1940	Ragi, Rice
156	6	1	3703	1250	Ragi, Rice
157	10	2	6286	1926	Ragi, Rice
159	14	—	5657	1736	Ragi
160	11	—	6972	2242	Ragi, Rice
161	10	—	4867	1589	Ragi
162	6	1	3893	1045	Ragi
163	8	—	3814	1465	Ragi
164	8	1	4358	1504	Ragi
165	8	1	4870	1487	Ragi
166	14	—	6558	1987	Ragi
167	9	2	5879	2171	Ragi
168	9	1	5211	1601	Ragi, Rice
169	14	—	8190	2613	Ragi, Rice
170	9	—	2681	708	Ragi, Rice
171	12	—	4343	1524	Ragi, Rice
172	7	1	4177	1407	Ragi, Rice
173	8	1	4529	1427	Ragi
174	7	1	4839	1677	Ragi, Rice
175	7	2	3295	947	Ragi, Rice

1	2	3	4	5	6
176	11	1	4447	1352	Ragi, Rice
177	9	—	5670	2384	Ragi
178	14	—	6981	2356	Ragi
180	9	2	3755	1156	Ragi, Rice
181	13	2	5193	1520	Ragi, Rice
182	12	1	4133	1208	Ragi, Rice
183	14	2	3958	1111	Ragi
184	7	1	2189	807	Ragi, Rice
185	10	1	3638	1036	Ragi, Rice
186	5	—	2397	643	Ragi, Rice
187	11	—	3687	1229	Ragi
188	11	—	5340	1669	Ragi
189	11	1	8227	2621	Ragi, Rice
190	11	—	9467	2972	Ragi
191	8	—	3551	861	Ragi
192	8	2	4135	1703	Ragi, Rice
193	7	—	4809	1612	Ragi, Rice
194	10	—	4099	2522	Ragi, Rice
195	7	—	2560	685	Ragi, Rice
196	8	1	6627	1959	Ragi, Rice
197	9	—	5189	1583	Ragi, Rice

(Contd.)

1	2	3	4	5	6
198	8	1	8954	2744	Ragi, Rice
199	6	—	5556	2104	Ragi, Rice
200	10	—	7245	2221	Ragi
201	5	—	3166	1019	Ragi
202	6	—	4333	1495	Ragi, Rice
5a	6	—	6017	1418	Oilseeds, Jowar
5b	7	—	6128	2402	Oilseeds, Jowar
5c	3	—	2864	1477	Oilseeds, Millets
5d	4	—	2903	1343	Oilseeds, Jowar
5e	6	—	3946	1770	Oilseeds, Jowar
7a	6	—	7817	3367	Multicrop
7b	3	1	2661	1152	Multicrop
7c	4	—	5699	2330	Multicrop
7d	6	—	4084	1631	Multicrop
7e	5	—	4087	1521	Oilseeds, Jowar
29a	6	—	6385	2208	Millets, Ragi
29b	4	1	4675	1590	Ragi, Millets
29c	5	—	5209	1961	Millets, Ragi
29d	3	—	1125	352	Millets, Ragi
29e	12	2	7294	2708	Ragi, Millets
51a	15	—	7159	2749	Oilseeds, Ragi, Rice

1	2	3	4	5	6
51b	9	3	3068	1067	Oilseeds, Ragi, Rice
51c	9	—	3827	1655	Oilseeds, Ragi, Rice
51d	4	—	3397	1062	Ragi, Oilseeds
51e	4	2	1242	657	Oilseeds, Ragi
71a	10	1	2738	946	Ragi
71b	5	2	3365	1113	Oilseeds, Ragi
71c	9	1	4991	1638	Oilseeds, Ragi
71d	8	1	2432	821	Ragi, Oilseeds
71e	8	1	2733	1048	Oilseeds, Ragi
71f	11	3	6393	2370	Ragi, Oilseeds
71g	9	1	3889	2350	Oilseeds, Ragi
108a	6	2	2173	778	Ragi
108b	5	2	1460	564	Ragi
108c	9	2	3298	1049	Ragi
108d	4	—	1404	418	Ragi
108e	8	—	4493	1472	Ragi
108f	7	—	3623	1289	Ragi
114a	5	2	1388	585	Ragi, Rice
114b	16	4	9930	3291	Ragi, Rice
114c	11	1	4853	1601	Ragi, Rice

(*Contd.*)

1	2	3	4	5	6
114d	4	2	1077	422	Ragi, Oilseeds
114e	11	—	5417	1767	Ragi, Rice
114f	12	1	8161	2327	Ragi, Rice
114g	3	2	2555	783	Ragi
114h	10	2	5803	1899	Ragi
114i	8	—	4268	1702	Ragi, Rice
114j	7	1	5414	1760	Ragi, Rice
114k	11	1	11 399	3531	Ragi, Rice
114 l	16	4	17.511	4721	Ragi, Rice
114m	5	—	2732	926	Ragi, Rice
114n	11	—	5790	1735	Ragi, Rice
114o	17	—	11,906	3952	Ragi, Rice
114p	5	—	4031	1472	Ragi, Rice
114q	5	—	829	252	Ragi, Rice
114r	10	—	5077	1483	Ragi, Rice
114s	7	—	2994	937	Ragi, Rice
114t	9	—	3727	1227	Ragi, Oilseeds, Rice
119a	5	—	1936	488	Ragi
119b	8	1	3385	731	Ragi, Rice
119c	5	1	3462	1011	Ragi, Rice
119d	6	—	2673	850	Ragi, Rice
119e	5	—	3688	1163	Ragi, Millets
119f	6	1	4689	1433	Ragi
119g	4	—	2303	910	Ragi, Rice
130a	6	—	2962	938	Ragi

1	2	3	4	5	6
130b	5	—	2008	605	Ragi
130c	4	—	2394	688	Ragi, Millets
130d	3	1	1212	384	Ragi, Jowar
130e	8	—	7022	2316	Ragi, Jowar
130f	8	—	5301	1577	Ragi, Rice
130g	10	—	2914	986	Ragi, Rice
130h	10	—	5577	1790	Ragi
140a	7	—	2779	820	Ragi, Millets
140b	4	—	1960	627	Ragi, Millets
140c	7	1	3457	1109	Ragi, Rice, Jowar
140d	7	3	5563	7774	Ragi
140e	5	2	1625	529	Ragi
140f	8	1	3393	1147	Ragi, Rice
158a	7	—	4538	1581	Ragi
158b	6	—	5244	1845	Ragi
158c	3	1	1291	399	Ragi, Rice
158d	6	2	4914	1653	Ragi, Rice
158e	6	—	2978	1045	Ragi, Rice
158f	6	—	3599	1112	Ragi, Rice
158g	4	—	2754	877	Ragi
179a	6	1	3502	1384	Ragi, Rice
179b	9	—	5781	1908	Ragi, Rice
179c	5	3	4920	1675	Ragi, Rice
179d	8	—	5115	1693	Ragi, Rice
179e	13	1	8263	2582	Ragi, Rice
179f	7	2	3508	1190	Ragi, Rice.

Appendix III

Central Places—Population, Functions and Composite Score

Sl. No.	Centres	LC No.	Taluk	Population (1971)	MS	SS	PO	TO	Med.	Weekly market	Composite score
1	2	3	4	5	6	7	8	9	10	11	12
1.	Tumkur	—	Tumkur	70476	1	1	1	1	1	1	142.08
2.	Tiptur	—	Tiptur	22592	1	1	1	1	1	1	59.95
3.	Sira	—	Sira	18299	1	1	1	1	1	1	52.58
4.	Madhugiri	—	Madhugiri	14117	1	1	1	1	1	1	45.41
5.	Kunigal	—	Kunigal	13437	1	1	1	1	1	1	44.24
6.	C.N. Halli	—	C.N. Halli	13061	1	1	1	1	1	1	43.59
7.	Gubbi	—	Gubbi	9537	1	1	1	1	1	1	37.55
8.	Pavagada	—	Pavagada	9004	1	1	1	1	1	1	36.64
9.	Turuvekere	—	Turuvekere	6536	1	1	1	1	1	1	32.40
10.	Y.N. Hoskore	—	Pavagada	6177	1	1	1	1	1	1	31.79
11.	Koratgere	—	Koratgere	5794	1	1	1	1	1	1	31.03
12.	Huliyar	136	C.N. Halli	6491	1	1	1	1	1	1	27.84
13.	Kyatsandara	112	Tumkur	4912	1	1	1	1	1	1	25.13
14.	Honnavalli	69	Tiptur	4489	1	1	1	1	1	1	24.40
15.	Amrutur	190	Kunigal	4455	1	1	1	1	1	1	24.35
16.	Huliyurdurga	134	Kunigal	5519	1	1	1	1	1	0	24.07

1	2	3	4	5	6	7	8	9	10	11	12
17.	Ammasandra	—	Turuvekere	1577	1	1	1	1	1	1	23.83
18.	Nadur	205	Sira	4127	1	1	1	1	1	1	23.78
19.	Kodagenhalli	87	Madhugiri	4727	1	1	1	1	1	0	22.68
20.	Hebbur	197	Tumkur	3371	1	1	1	1	1	1	22.49
21.	Settikere	40	C.N. Halli	3296	1	1	1	1	1	1	22.35
22.	Nonavinakere	199	Tiptur	3205	1	1	1	1	1	1	22.20
23.	Kallambella	52	Sira	3134	1	1	1	1	1	1	22.08
24.	Chelur	286	Gubbi	2951	1	1	1	1	1	1	21.77
25.	Holavanhalli	48	Koratgere	4222	1	1	1	1	1	0	21.75
26.	Timrachahalli	199	C.N. Halli	3791	1	1	1	1	1	0	21.22
27.	Mayasandra	126	Turuvekere	2468	1	1	1	1	1	1	20.94
28.	Kellur	132	Gubbi	3176	1	1	1	0	1	1	20.56
29.	Hosakere	28	Madhugiri	2187	1	1	1	1	1	1	20.46
30.	Dandinasivara	65	Turuvekere	2126	1	1	1	1	1	1	20.35
31.	Midigeshi	1	Madhugiri	2033	1	1	1	1	1	1	20.19
32.	Bellavi	275	Tumkur	1984	1	1	1	1	1	1	20.11
33.	Itakadibbanahalli	53	Madhugiri	3208	1	1	1	1	1	0	20.01
34.	Handanekere	80	C.N. Halli	2333	1	1	1	0	1	1	19.97
35.	Kadaba	89	Gubbi	2640	1	1	1	0	1	1	19.64
36.	Byalya	164	Madhugiri	2414	1	1	1	0	1	1	19·25
37.	Honnudike	365	Tumkur	2131	1	1	1	0	1	1	18.77

(Contd.)

1	2	3	4	5	6	7	8	9	10	11	12
38.	Chandrasekharapura	53	Gubbi	2432	1	1	1	1	1	0	18.68
39.	Nagavalli	233	Turuvekere	2433	1	1	1	1	1	0	18.68
40.	Urdigere	63	Tumkur	2365	1	1	1	1	1	0	18.56
41.	Nittur	152	Gubbi	2307	1	1	1	1	0	1	18.53
42.	Banasandra	30	Turuvekere	1975	1	1	1	0	1	1	18.50
43.	Tavarekere	176	Sira	1915	1	1	1	0	1	1	18.40
44.	Nagasandra	299	Kunigal	1821	1	1	1	0	1	1	18.24
45.	Baragur	218	Sira	1758	1	1	1	0	1	1	18.13
46.	Kolala	144	Koratgere	1610	1	1	1	0	1	1	17.88
47.	Bukkapatna	100	Sira	4098	1	0	1	0	1	1	17.52
48.	Mavinakere	234	Turuvekere	1543	1	1	1	0	1	1	17.07
49.	Hattidurga	93	Kunigal	1020	1	1	1	0	1	1	16.86
50.	Baladhara	184	Tumkur	786	1	1	1	0	1	1	16.46
51.	Gulur	328	Tumkur	3114	1	1	1	1	0	0	15.43
52.	*Ujjani*	160	Kunigal	2877	1	0	1	0	1	1	15.34
53.	Rampur	50	Koratgere	2751	1	0	1	0	1	1	15.21
54.	Tirumani	123	Pavagada	1229	1	1	1	1	1	0	14.32
55.	Mangalavada	55	Pavagada	1978	1	1	1	0	1	0	14.02
56.	Sampige	85	Turuvekere	1969	1	1	1	0	0	1	13.98
57.	Hagalavadi	232	Gubbi	3185	1	1	1	0	1	0	13.73
58.	Neralekere	28	Madhugiri	1789	1	1	1	0	0	1	13.61
59.	Bidare	308	Gubbi	1806	1	0	1	0	1	1	13.59

1	2	3	4	5	6	7	8	9	10	11	12
60.	Badavanalli	317	Madhugiri	1734	1	0	1	0	1	1	13.47
61.	Tandaga	213	Turuvekere	1645	1	0	1	0	1	1	13.32
62.	Kotta	46	Sira	2554	1	0	1	0	1	0	12.74
63.	Doddaguni	218	Gubbi	1183	1	1	1	0	0	1	12.65
64.	Kandikere	193	C.N. Halli	2483	1	1	1	0	0	0	12.62
65.	Mathighatta	113	C.N. Halli	1155	1	1	1	0	0	1	12.61
66.	Bevinahalli	201	Sira	2465	1	0	1	0	1	0	12.59
67.	Edinahalli	2	Tiptur	2692	1	0	1	1	0	0	12.44
68.	Mavinahalli	79	Gubbi	1118	1	0	1	0	1	1	12.41
69.	Karikere	53	Tiptur	1076	1	0	1	0	1	1	12.34
70.	Alaleghatta	258	Gubbi	2342	1	1	1	0	1	0	12.23
71.	Tarur	70	Sira	2266	1	1	1	0	0	0	12.25
72.	Kondethimmanahalli	57	Pavagada	2327	1	1	0	0	1	0	11.94
73.	Magodu	7	Sira	1963	1	0	1	0	1	0	11.73
74.	Tovinakere	230	Koratgere	1957	1	1	1	0	0	0	11.72
75.	Muganayakanakote	164	Gubbi	1897	1	0	1	0	1	0	11.62
76.	Kottagada	41	Pavagada	1847	1	0	1	0	1	0	11.53
77.	Yadiyur	251	Kunigal	818	1	1	1	1	0	0	11.49
78.	Dommathamari	10	Pavagada	1682	1	0	1	0	1	0	11.25
79.	Kanekere	192	C.N. Halli	4252	1	1	0	0	0	0	11.17
80.	Bajagoor	220	Tiptur	1578	1	0	1	0	0	1	11.07

(Contd.)

1	2	3	4	5	6	7	8	9	10	11	12
81.	Biligere	140	Tiptur	1538	1	0	1	0	1	0	11.00
82.	Gonitumkur	227	Turuvekere	1488	1	0	1	0	1	0	10.92
83.	Kethigere	52	Kunigal	1459	1	0	1	0	1	0	10.87
84.	Baluvaneralu	87	Tiptur	1422	1	0	1	0	0	1	10.80
85.	Hosur	194	Sira	1299	1	0	1	0	0	1	10.59
86.	Kubbahalli	141	Tiptur	1275	1	0	1	0	0	1	10.55
87.	Dobbeghatta	190	Turuvekere	1326	1	0	1	1	0	0	10.54
88.	Kanathur	203	Turuvekere	1225	1	0	1	0	0	1	10.47
89.	Yadavanne	202	Kunigal	1215	1	1	1	0	0	0	10.45
90.	Guligenahalli	17	Sira	1186	1	0	1	0	0	1	10.40
91.	Seethakal	68	Tumkur	1178	1	0	1	0	1	0	10.38
92.	Hendere	205	Sira	3777	1	0	1	0	0	0	10.35
93.	Sugur	197	Tiptur	1116	1	0	1	0	1	0	10.26
94.	Horagere	214	Sira	1041	1	0	1	0	0	1	10.15
95.	Byadanoor	26	Pavagada	3614	1	0	1	0	0	0	10.07

Note : MS : Middle School; SS : Secondary School; PO : Post Office;
TO : Telegraph Office; Med : Medical Facilities.

Appendix IV

Tumkur Project : Objectives and Work

Tumkur Project, a study on rural development located in the Tumkur District of Karnataka, was initiated in November 1976, under the guidance of Professor V.K.R.V. Rao, who is the Honorary Director of the Project. The Project has three main objectives. First, the Project brought together a group of researchers drawn from the different units in the Institute for Social and Economic Change with the intention of building up an inter-disciplinary team of researchers working in close co-operation with each other and looking at the problems of rural development from a common perspective delineated by the Hon. Director in collaboration with the team. Second, the issues relating to human resources and to the role of rural communities, social groups and institutions in rural development were to form the principal theme underlying and motivating the studies undertaken in the Project; the larger and long-term objective was to try to accumulate a body of knowledge on the theme which could both help policy-makers in field, and also, contribute fresh and relevant insights on the theme to social sciences concerned with rural development. Consistent with this objective, the third objective of the Project was to prepare a data base capable of supporting a wide range of studies besides those undertaken within and during the duration of the Project.

The field work of the Project was conducted in April-June 1977. It covered 245 villages in Tumkur, a 10 per cent sample of inhabited villages in the district. The data were collected with the help of about 250 village-level and block-level officers and an equal number of school teachers who worked under the guidance and supervision of the members of the Project team. Two schedules were used for the field-work—(i) a comprehensive village questionnaire covering agriculture and land-use, other economic activities, rural amenities and services and village level institutions—Panchayat, Co-operative Society, School and Voluntary Organisations; and (ii) an eight-page household schedule—canvassed with each resident household in the sample village and covering a total of over 30,000 households—focussed on the socio-economic status and life-style as reflected in caste, occupation, ownership of land, housing, membership of and access to institutions, contacts outside village and indicators of health and education. The principal data base of the Project consists of village and household data for sample villages and village-wise population census (from 1941 to 1971) and agricultural census (1970) data for all villages in the district. Arrangements are being made to put these data on computer tapes to ensure their ready availability for future research use.

During the period August 1977 to October 1978, the Project team prepared a set of preliminary papers based on secondary and village-questionnaire data. The set consists of ten taluk profiles—one for each taluk in the district—and a paper each on demographic change and villages in Tumkur. The findings and insights of these papers have been brought together in a synoptic theme paper prepared by the Honorary Director entitled "Issues and Problems of Development of Tumkur". These papers were presented to and formed the principal source material for the four-week Workshop on Population Planning and Area Development organised by the United Nations Asian and Pacific Development Institute, Bangkok in collaboration with the Institute for Social and Economic Change and held in November-December 1978 at the Institute campus in Bangalore. The workshop was attended by twenty participants drawn from eight countries of the South Asian region and the members of the Project team were among the faculty and resource persons of the workshop. The key output of the workshop was a medium-term development plan for Tumkur prepared by the participants with the help of the workshop personnel.

Concurrently with the preliminary papers, work was also initiated on a number of theme-oriented studies, some completed and others in progress. They form the substantive output of the project and they are being brought out in a series—Studies in Integrated Rural Development—under the general editorship of Professor V.K.R.V. Rao. The time schedule to which the team is working is to complete these studies before the termination of the Project in November 1980. The tentative titles listed below would give a broad idea about the focus and content of these studies.

1. Rural Development and Village : Perspectives for Planning for Development (completed)
2. Panchayats and Rural Development (completed)
3. Planning Unit Areas for Integrated Rural Development—An Exercise (completed)
4. School Education in Rural Areas—A Case Study of Tumkur District (completed)
5. Dimensions of Backwardness in Pavagada Taluk (completed)
6. Human Factors in Rural Development (planned)
7. Micro-Level Planning for Rural Development—An Application of Cluster approach (completed)

These studies are visualised as the beginning of a research programme on rural development consisting of different but converging lines of investigation. The lines of investigation are expected to be pursued further—and fresh lines added—by the different units in the Institute for Social and Economic Change beyond the period of the project. A beginning has already been made in this direction by the Social Service Management, Rural Economics and Education Units which are in the process of proposing studies based wholly or in part on Tumkur Project data. There is some ground to hope that this larger research programme will provide opportunities and incentives to different social science disciplines in the Institute to come closer and pool their insights on the analytical and policy aspects of rural development. Such pooling of insights, in its turn, could initiate a trend towards inter-disciplinary research growing out of shared and interacting perspectives of individual social science disciplines and, in the process, acquiring a holistic perspective richer and more perceptive than its components. This is looking much too far ahead but it is precisely the lure of this distant goal which persuaded the Institute for Social and Economic Change to make a beginning with the Tumkur Project.

Index